Stolen Treasure

The horrendous environmental and ecological scandals that are destroying the natural heritage of Eastern Canada and the United States.

by Peter Dube

authorHOUSE®

AuthorHouse™
1663 Liberty Drive, Suite 200
Bloomington, IN 47403
www.authorhouse.com
Phone: 1-800-839-8640

First published by AuthorHouse 4/6/2009

ISBN: 978-1-4389-6564-2 (sc)

Library of Congress Control Number: 2009902862

Printed in the United States of America
Bloomington, Indiana

This book is printed on acid-free paper.

Cover photo Dr. Paul Leblanc

DEDICATIONS:

I dedicate this book to my late Uncle Jean Paul Dubé, an outstanding conservationist and salmon angler.J P believed that one should never back down when confronting wrong doing.He thought us to stand-up and fight when you know you are right.

Since I am not a professional writer, I will always be grateful to a wonderful generous person and a close friend Charlene Moores, for her help in writing the foundation for this document.Also from a long time friend and fishing partner Robert Schyberg who contributed material on the early history of the Restigouche and served editor of this book.

This book would not have been possible without the substantial information contribution granted by friends and clients from around the globe, many of whom are dedicated to achieving a cleaner environment and restoring a sustainable habitat for the King of Fish.

Together we work, fight and pray that The Atlantic Salmon may find a way to flourish as a wild species and return once again in great numbers to our rivers and streams as they once did, prior to being decimated by the forest industry and corrupt government policy.Our goal must be to achieve not only survivability and sustainability for The Atlantic Salmon, but also returning a bountiful economic resource that has been stolen from the people of Canada.We look to the current Pacific Ocean Salmon resource as a measurement of what has been lost on the Atlantic side; billions of dollars, thousands of jobs, an entire economy, and a National Treasure.

Acknowledgement

This book is written as a result of a heritage bequeathed by a man for whom the wellbeing of Atlantic salmon took precedence over his own.I am extremely grateful to my late Uncle John Paul Dubé, for the heritage he has left me.A long time friend and fishing companion, author of many books, (Lets Save Our Salmon) on salmon conservation and fishing techniques, John Paul was a very well informed and dedicated salmon angler, and genuine conservationist.As co-ordinator of Quebec salmon rivers, he was a bank of information.

His passion for fly fishing; his relentless pursuit to do what was right to protect the hunting and fishing heritage his father (J. Albert, outfitter for salmon, trout, moose, deer, caribou, and black bear since 1906, throughout the Gaspé peninsula. See map of territory at end of book.) left him, and his strong conviction to save our salmon.All of which will remain with us, for as long as Salmo Solar continues to return to our rivers.

Inspired by the profound conservationist example he has instilled in me, it is my belief . . . that the legacy must continue!

Introduction

This document emerges from my deep concern for the Restigouche River, which is literally being destroyed by uncontrolled Clear-cutting, that goes on with hardly a word of disapproval; even from people who should be most concerned.Are they all muzzled, like Dr. David Suzuki? (See letter in later chapter)Or is it that no one is aware of what is happening to our forest and rivers?Presently, it is just about impossible to inform the general public of the activities that are taking place in our forests, because most of the media is under siege, closely scrutinised and controlled when it comes to transmitting clear-cutting information by radio or TV.

This work is put forth with the hope that it will strum some sensitive chord deep inside of you, awakening the urge to do something . . . Now!We cannot depend upon our governments, nor upon the elite of this country . . . They are part of the problem . . . not the solution!Whatever the reason for our complacency, we cannot afford to let things go on as they are.Our rivers and forests will not stand this abuse much longer without being subject to crippling, irreversible damage.If each of us does not do our part to bring clear-cutting under control, then . . . Who will?

Pete Dubé

November 1995

ATTENTION:

Please be advised: The declarations in this book are **WITHOUT PREJUDICE** and **only** reflect the author's personal opinion.

Contents

Chapter One

The Great Restigouche River Basin . . .

In the course of reading this book you will become acquainted with several rivers in eastern Canada.One river in particular, The Restigouche, carries a certain mystique that is hard to explain.Everyone who experiences her haunting beauty seems captivated by a magical spell and the memory of this enchantment is imprinted deep within the mind and spirit..Flowing between lush green mountains with a meandering, almost musical rhythm, and twisting through the dark forests separating Quebec and New Brunswick, the fabulous Restigouche River is probably the world's greatest Atlantic Salmon River and an irreplaceable national treasure of Canada.. Unchanged through countless millennium witnessed only by the annual pilgrimages of Aboriginal Peoples, coinciding with the annual migrations of salmon, this incomparable river has, in more recent times, suffered horrendous environmental destruction at the hands of giant forestry operations.Today we find The Restigouche under serious environmental threat and at the center of an intense social, ecological, and economic battle regarding the future of Atlantic Canada.

Just a little bit of Geography and History:

The village of Matapédia is located at the junction of the Matapédia and the Restigouche Rivers. For thousands of years the flow of water from these two rivers has functioned as the environmental heart and center for The Atlantic Salmon species in North America.

Matapédia is part of the immense territory (from St John River to Temiscouata and the whole Gaspé Peninsula) occupied by the Algonquin Indian culture, primarily Micmac tribal groups, many centuries before the arrival of the white people.Matapédia is a Micmac name meaning"meeting of the waters". Truly named because it is here that the Restigouche and the Matapédia Rivers join together forming a flow of water which commands a world-wide reputation for salmon fishing second to none.

Starting around 1609 and continuing for the next 150 years Jesuit missionaries following the early explorations of Samuel sieur de Champlain made the first maps of the region. More white people appeared in our region in five successive waves. First, were the Loyalists, refugees from the United States, who had originally come from Scotland and settled in New England.They fled north to this region, following the American Revolutionary War and arrived in the early 1800s.Later, groups of French speaking Acadians arrived around 1860, having been forced from their original maritime landholdings by the British authorities.The Irish arrived about 1870.The fifth group, of English origin, appeared about 1875 after completion of the Inter-Colonial Railway.Finally, French Canadian families from villages along the St. Lawrence River settled in the region.Different in background, language and religion, these five groups were greatly helped through the years by the beneficial influence of the clergy, both Protestant and Catholic.Just like Canada, Matapédia has had constantly to take into consideration the great diversity of its inhabitants.Through Bilingualism and co-operation, we live together in harmony and fraternity.

The early settlers soon realized the potential of the river valley for farming, as the land is extremely rich and relatively free of rocks.In the early 1880`s small portions of forest were cleared for farming miles away from the river on the highland plateau's.Settlers slowly moved in. They gradually formed the population of approximately nine thousand residents that we have today.They located upstream on the plateaus of the Restigouche River above Matapédia.Farming, logging and salmon fishing provided a living for these people.

It is not surprising the avid practitioners of the Salmon Fishing arts were attracted to our rivers very early on and from far away.Even before the existence of a highway and a railway, they came to enjoy the irresistible thrill of luring that royal fish, the delight of the most discriminating gourmet, the enchantment of the elite of fishermen.No obstacle could stop them from searching the "silvery treasures" of the rivers.They would come by "steamboat" to Dalhousie or through the Saint John River and would portage through vast sections of forest to their destination.

The Restigouche Salmon Club, the most prestigious private club in the world, was founded in 1880.Through the years, the club entertained as members and guests many world-famous people from Canada and the United States.Due to this, Matapédia was known as "The Salmon Capital of the World".Among our many distinguished visitors were members of the Royal Family: Princess Louise of England; King Edward the VII; the Duke and Dutchess of Windsor; athlete Jack Dempsey; actor Bing Crosby and most US presidents.Fishing camps, some of them very attractive buildings, were built on the banks of our rivers.Very rich fishermen came by train.Some had their own private car on the siding in front of the station and were served on board by their own staff. Some even brought their wives, accompanied by a nurse, a hairdresser, and sometime a doctor.At the Restigouche Hotel we see fishermen using one room for himself, another room where his meals are served, one room for his chauffer and another for his secretary.Other virtuosos of salmon fishing have barges (large scows) fit up like little floating palaces that are towed up river by horses.We can imagine the host and his guest lolling in their armchair on the rear deck, admiring the beauties of a virgin natural paradise passing by their eyes; stopping as they pleased for a period of fishing or for peaceful night sleep in the quiet of the forest, gently rocked by the lapping of waves.

A Team of Horses Towing a Scow on a Tributary of the Restigouche River

I guess it was only a matter of a short time before instinct and human nature ran its course causing these individuals to want to own this paradise for themselves and to keep others out. This desire drove them to petition the government for exclusive "rights" to the fishing pools along the river. Over the next century and a half ordinary citizens of Canada would learn a great deal about these so called "Riparian Rights" and in the following chapters the problems caused by the granting of these rights will be discussed in detail. Thus, the decision by the Privy Council in 1880 to grant fishing rights to riparian owners originated our present system of river exploitation. The owners of land bordering the rivers were interested in selling "rights" while at the same time keeping their land as the sale of only one fishing rod in depth of frontage land was sufficient to transfer the fishing rights. This decision triggered a virtual "treasure hunt" for the fishing rights on our rivers.

The Matapedia River . . .

It was then that Lord Mount Stephen acquired all the fishing rights from Causapscal to the Assemetquagan River, building his famous Matamajaw camp at the mouth of the Causapscal River. Son of a Scottish carpenter, Stephen arrived in Montreal in 1850, at the age of twenty-one started a business, got rich and became president of the Bank of Montreal. In 1881, as the McDonald government was looking for funds and a contractor bold enough to build a railway linking Canada from East to West, Stephen took up the challenge and formed a company with Donald A. Smith, his cousin, and James J. Hill. The name of the company was Canadian Pacific Railway and this gigantic project was completed in six years.

In gratitude, Stephen was made a baron with the title of Lord Mount Stephen, and Donald Smith a baron with the title of Lord Strathcona. The three of them became members of the Restigouche Salmon Club and Lord Strathcona had a residence in Matapédia, just in front of the Restigouche Hotel. In 1880, John S. Kennedy, a New York banker, acquired some parcels of land from Lord Mount Stephen and some other rights to the Camp Glenn Emma, named in honour of his wife. During that period, a group of forty financiers and members of the American elite met in New York to establish the official rules and form the original membership of the exclusive and world renowned Restigouche Salmon Club (RSC). (In the following chapters we will have a chance to learn a great deal about current membership and operations of this club but for now, it will prove interesting and even entertaining to remain, for a short time, in our historical perspective.)

In a short period, thanks to unlimited financial resources, these supermen of American business acquired all the fishing rights of any value on both our rivers and most of the land in the Village of Matapédia and surroundings, plus all the properties of Lord Mount Stephen. Who were these "Supermen"? Well, the list of their names can be found in any book on American history because they were the founders of today's mega-banks and industrial empires. They commanded staggering wealth in the years leading up to the turn of the 20th century and these men, like the magnificent Atlantic Salmon they prized so dearly, began to return year after year to the rivers of their enchantment. Let's continue:

Another fishing club was formed when J. B. Cobb, president of American Tobacco, and A. H. Cosden bought the rights of Alexander of Matapédia and Mann's Pool from the Restigouche Salmon Club. They built the superb Cold Spring Camp. Subsequently, this property was owned by W.E. Corey, president of U.S. Steel and then, by George Washington Hill, Cobb's son-in-law, to whom he succeeded as president of The American Tobacco Company. Incidentally, Mr. Hill was the man who spent fifty million dollars in one year to publicize the Lucky Strike cigarette, serving as real life prototype to the American film "The Hucksters".

The subsequent owners of the Cold Spring Camp were Mr. Andrew A. Fraser, well known New York lawyer; John G. Martin, hero of the American Air Force and important financier of Hartford, Connecticut.Now, this property has returned into the hands of the Hill family.

In 1910, Fred K. Barbour acquired from the Restigouche Salmon Club all that is now part of the Tobique Salmon Club, where he built a beautiful lodge.Later on, this property was owned by A. G. Walwyn and Major Hahn.

Later on The Restigouche River . . .

As discussed earlier, the decision by the Privy Council of Canada to grant fishing rights to riparian owners triggered a frantic race to acquire fishing privileges on the Restigouche River.The Restigouche Salmon Club got the lion's share.But, many other interested parties were also in the running and fishing camps began to appear all along the river.Many of these camps were sumptuous lodges built in harmony with their picturesque surroundings; some were planned by Sanford White, a member of the Restigouche Salmon Club and a famous architect.

One must canoe down the river to really appreciate how large and beautiful the Restigouche is; how picturesque the sites at every curve of the river.

The Restigouche Salmon Club owns five camps on the banks of the river; Downs Gulch and Red Bank up-stream the Patapedia; Indian House, built by White; Pine Island and Cheaters Brook. Each one accommodates four "sports" plus the staff: one cook and one valet for the guest; a man of all work; eight guides (two guides per fisherman) and a cook for the staff.

The other fishing camps along the Restigouche are listed in order, from the mouth of the Kedgwick River and downstream from there:

First there is Rogers Club, a beautiful camp created by architect White.Next, England's Flat, just downstream of Indian House.At Tom's Brook we find the camp of the McConnell family of Montreal.Mr. J. W. McConnell was a generous philanthropist, giving out more than one hundred million in his lifetime and leaving a foundation now valued at more than six hundred million.Further down the river, we come to Red Pine, a fishing camp administered by Senator Pirie of Grand Falls.

Toad Brook is owned by the Goelet family of New York, with four generations on the Restigouche River.Their two first camps were burned down by forest fires.The foundations of the last one can be seen next to the brook.It was a lodge of exceptional beauty.After the last fire, Mr. Goelet acquired the superb Camp Albany, which he still owns. He belongs to a prestigious family that traces its original land holdings on Manhattan Island, NY back to a grant from King George III of England before the American Revolution.This land today surrounds Rockefeller Center which they still own.They are founding members of the Restigouche Salmon Club.

The magnificent Brandy Brook Camp is another creation of architect White.It is a huge building rising above a gentle slope, featuring a well-groomed lawn landscaped with a great variety of flowers.The Brandy Brook sings gently through the property before flowing into the large and deep pool that faces the camp.It is one of the most picturesque spots on the Restigouche River.Mr. Robert Lehman, the great American financier, is the owner.

A little further down, we find the Deeside Lodge, now deserted, formerly owned by the Strauss family, owners of the famous Macy's stores in New York.

At the confluence of the Upsulquitch and the Restigouche Rivers, sitting on the hillside, architect Stanford White designed a superb Lodge, with a fantastic view as far as the eye can reach upstream and downstream on both rivers.This is Camp Harmony, founded by Dean Sage, who wrote in 1887: "The Restigouche and its Salmon Fishing", a book in great request, valued at $2,500.00 as of 1975.A new edition now sells at $500.00 a copy.The author died at Camp Harmony in 1902 and so did his son, Dean Sage Jr., while fishing there in 1943.Four generations of the Sage family have owned that camp.

The next camp is Runnymede Lodge, for a long time the property of Alan Lehman, member of the aforementioned family of investment bankers, it is now the property of Joseph Cullman the 3rd, of The Philip Morris Tobacco Company and Kraft Foods.

At Moore's Settlement, we find Grog Island Camp, for many years the property of Jos. Pulitzer of the St. Louis Post Dispatch, donator of the famous Pulitzer Prize for Journalism, Literature and Arts.

Further down the river, at Flatlands, is located The Brunswick Lodge, for a long time the property of I. W. Killiam of Montreal, member of the Restigouche Salmon Club.President of Royal Securities, he died while fishing nearby on the Grand Cascapedia River.Mr. Killam was immensely rich but rather austere.However his wife knew what to do with that money.She died in 1965 in a villa on the French Riviera, acquired from Count Giovani Angelli, owner of the Fiat Company, for three million dollars.Her personal jewelry alone was valued at four million.A baseball enthusiast, she offered, in 1956, the extravagant sum of six million dollars to prevent the Dodgers from moving to Los Angeles.

There is no question that the list of members and former members of the RSC shows the enormous power, influence and wealth that these famous American families brought to the area.One very wealthy American president, Chester A. Arthur, was also a salmon fishing enthusiast. After leaving the White House in 1886 he became President of the Restigouche Salmon Club in 1887 and died the same year from complications of pneumonia caught while on a fishing trip.His dear friend and fellow New Yorker, Louis Comfort Tiffany, the foremost art designer of his day and founder of the most prestigious glass and jewelry studio in the world, was also a member of the Club.Chester A. Arthur was so extravagant that when he assumed occupancy of the White House, he had most of the original furniture (some of it dating back to Washington and Adams) hauled out and burned. It was replaced by furniture purchased from and designed and created by his friend Tiffany.

We also have stories about other Presidents, Secretaries of State, great novelists, war hero, and great inventors among others.We could go on and on with stories about the rich and famous RSC members but this is supposed to be only a brief history, so we will limit the gossip to one more really good story, an interesting event concerning two members of the Restigouche Salmon Club, and the death of the great architect Stanford White (who built most fishing camps on the Restigouche River), killed by Harry K. Thaw on June the 25th 1906 at the First Madison Square Garden in the Rooftop Theatre.

Mr. Harry K. Thaw an extremely rich man, was married to Evelyn Nesbit one of the most popular American actress and model at the time. She was also involved in a love affair with Stanford White. Architect White was well known as a "Ladies Man" and had an apartment next to the First Madison Square Garden. The bedroom was equipped with mirrors on the ceiling above the bed, an open bathtub, a bar and a red velvet swing.It served as the real life prototype for the American film produced in 1955 "The Girl in the Red Velvet Swing". Mr. White even had a salmon fly designed for him, it was named: "The Night Hawk".

While Mr. Thaw was fishing up river at Indian House (camp of the RSC) on the Restigouche at the end of the day on June the 23rd, 1906, Mr. Thaw received a telegram by the mail boat postal service, (two men poling a 26 foot canoe by river to Indian House, 39 miles upstream from Matapedia.)No one to this day knows what was written on the telegram, but early the next morning Mr. Thaw and his two Indians guides headed down river in their canoe to Matapedia.Mr. Thaw wanted to be on time to take the evening train to Montreal.On the 25th of June he arrived in New York City and that evening he went to the First Madison Square Garden where an evening was held in the Rooftop Theatre.Mr. White was present accompanied by Thaw's stunningly beautiful wife Evelyn. Insane from jealousy, Mr. Thaw approached Stanford White from behind and shot him three times in the head.

This incident became one of the longest and most expensive court cases of the century.Mr. Thaw pleaded not guilty by reason of insanity, and after having spent millions on his defense he was freed.A year later he was charged of having sexually assaulted and "horsewhipped" Fred B. Gubby Jr. a teen-age boy and was sent to asylum for 7 years.

The Meaning of the word Restigouche

The word Restigouche is a MicMac name and there are several interpretations of its meaning.We have adopted this one, as authenticated by Father Pacifique, a specialist in the MicMac language, who says the word Restigouche derives from "Listogotjg," a war cry meaning: "disobey your father."

The story is that, a long time before the arrival of the white people, a skirmish took place far up the Restigouche River, when a party of young MicMac "braves" waged war against the Mohawks, an Indian tribe from what is now upstate New York, who were poaching salmon in the best pools at the head of the Restigouche, during the spawning season.The young chief of the expedition launched forth on that adventure against the formal interdiction of his father, chief of the MicMac tribe.He got cause to rue it, because he was slaughtered with all his war party.This is why the river was baptized: "Restigouche."

The Restigouche River, Next Closest Place to Heaven . . .

As so well written in Al Carter's book, "The Restigouche, Next Closest Place to Heaven," riparian owners are so closely attached to this river it is unthinkable for them to share this heaven.To them all others are poachers, especially the local "peasants" bordering the riverbank.

Many club members and Riparian Rights Owners on the Restigouche are insanely attached to this river and its salmon fishing.Some of them have spent up to four generations closely hugging this little paradise all to themselves, just as if it was the next closest place to heaven.Many of these riparian owners have selected to spend their last days here, fishing to the very end, collapsing right on the riverbank while fishing for those Giant Silvery Treasures.

This extremely wealthy group of North American elite's would in my opinion take any action required for preserving and controlling for themselves all riparian rights and as much land as possible bordering the Restigouche River Basin.Controlling the land bordering the Restigouche River allowed the riparian owners to establish the kind of developments surrounding the river that suited them, at times even if choices were very detrimental to the economy of the region.

Description of the Restigouche River Basin:

The Restigouche River Basin has five tributaries the Matapédia, Upsalquitch, Patapédia, Kedgwick and the Little Main.

All five run through moderately elevated highland, reaching slightly more than two thousand feet in elevation.

The Restigouche is a fast running river, yet gentle.Its watershed is large; covering about one hundred miles in length and width, with very considerable water volume for a Salmon River.

One finds huge flatlands on the plateaus with very thick topsoil mostly covered by conifer forest.

The Restigouche is also a very fragile river; its gravel particles are smaller in size than a man`s fist. Nature gave the Restigouche River a tremendous water retention capacity for that reason.These physical descriptions are cited here to provide a backdrop for catastrophic events which will be discussed in chapters to come.

Logging on the Restigouche River Basin:

The crosscut saw was used for logging until about 1928.Men worked these saws in pairs, as a team of two good men was required to handle one of them.Horses were used to pull the logs out of the woods.

Teamster hauling pulpwood near the Restigouche

It was illegal at that time to cut trees smaller than **twelve inches** at the butt.The buck-saw made its appearance in the late twenties and was the tool to be used until the fifties, when chain saws were first heard screaming in our forests.With the advent of paper mills, smaller and smaller trees were now targeted and harvested by the millions of tons to provide fibre for the mills.Yet this was only to be the beginning of clear cut logging practices.

As early as the forties the logging industry was very well established here.The method, (until 1972 on the Restigouche River) was to float the logs out on the river, called the drive.Every spring after the freshet, some one hundred thousand cords of wood were dumped into the river.

Log Drives on a tributary of the Restigouche

At time bulldozers had to be used to push a logjam into smaller tributaries.Often dynamite was used . . . used as regular routine . . . no questions asked!

Bulldozer Working at Pushing a Log Drive Forward

In the sixties, unions were well established among forest workers and logging companies felt threatened and sought to find an alternative method of cutting lumber, and at the same time boost profits.

Heavy machinery was the answer.These machines made it possible to harvest greater amounts of wood in a fraction of the time.This new style of logging was the fatal blow, which would cripple the Restigouche River before the end of the twentieth century. By the late eighties the prime lumber of our forest were completely cut.Today we are cutting big portions of forest for the second or even the third time around.

In 1974 on the gin clear Nouvelle River (30 miles east of Matapédia) the New Brunswick International Paper Company did not like the way the Nouvelle River had previously performed during the last few pulp-drives.The N.B.I.P. with the legend Richard Nelson Adams as Forman for the job, decided to give it a face-lift, N.B.I.P. style!What was needed . . . a river that was straight, narrow and deep with a mega flat on the riverbank.So, the N.B.I.P. channelled the Nouvelle River with bulldozers on a stretch of about five kilometres, making sure it would include a mega flat that could accommodate some twenty thousand cords of pulpwood.

The N.B.I.P was charged for the incident, but charges were not initiated by the action of our Quebec Government, whose responsibility it was to look after these matters. If it had not been for a few offended individuals like, Jean Noel Landry who persisted in having the charges stick, it is evident that most likely nothing would have been done, especially since the records of our provincial Government in matters of environmental control shows their extreme lack of concern.

On the Assemetquagan River (tributary of the Matapédia River) from millage thirteen to millage five the river is completely flat, not a single pool to be counted.The balance of the river has a normal number of gin-clear deep pools.What intrigues me, is the fact that huge pulp dumping (ten thousand cords or more) were made from the landing flat at millage thirteen to where the bulldozers exited the pulp drive at camp road millage five. Most likely a similar situation as on the Nouvelle River took place on the Assemetquagan River.

The Nouvelle River (30 miles East of Matapedia) after a bulldozer's facelift

It is estimated to completely repair the Restigouche River Basin from erosion could cost a billion dollars and the same for the Miramichi River.Governments are well aware of the exorbitant cost involved to repair damaged rivers by eresponsible logging practice, onCanada and the US East Coast a hundred billion would not be enough to repair all of these rivers that are today in peril.

Let us put the whole picture together:

When heavy machinery enters the forest for logging, it not only removes the trees.It destroys the moss and compact the earth.You may have seen forest roads with water puddles that persist in remaining for weeks after the last rain.Why?Compacted ground!The ground is compacted by heavy trucks, cars and machinery, which cause it to lose its ability to absorb water.

The moss on the ground of a virgin conifer forest is similar to the insulation in the walls of your home.You have seen it…that pink stuff!There is nothing in that insulation but air! You can squeeze an eight-inch loaf to less than a half inch.How does it insulate?By trapping dead air…just like the moss in the forest does! Dead air is one of the best insulators known to man.And what else could help to protect the ground from freezing during the winter?Of course!Loose snow and the cover of trees!In clear cuttings, moss is completely crushed, thus losing its capacity to insulate.The ground is compacted, making it vulnerable to freezing many feet deep, particularly if snow is late in coming.

A Forest Destroyer COMPACTING a Plateau of the Restigouche River

The Forest Destroyer Working a Plateau of the Restigouche, leaving it unprotected from heavy rainfall that will transport massive erosion deposit to the river.

Wind speed at ground level will more than double in velocity in clear-cut openings, in contrast to wind velocity in the forest.(Cline, Haupt, and Campbell, June 1977.)

This wind increase transports the snow, making it wind packed.In the forest, trees act as snow-fences, keeping the snow from being transported; giving it much more fluff.This increases the protection of the ground against freezing in the extremely cold part of the winter, when the thermometer remains below zero F. for weeks at a time.Numerous studies clearly show that water yield (the amount of water from melting snow and ice which runs into the rivers) can dramatically increase by removing forest cover in all cases.(Goodel 1958; Hornsbeck et al. 1970; Hoover 1944; Hoyt and Troxell 1934; Johnson and Kroner 1956; Lewis 1968; Love 1955; Mortinelli 1964; McGuinness and Harold 1971; Patrick and Reinhart 1971; Rich et al. 1961; Rich 1972; Shooner, groupe Salar 1992; and Plamondon A. 1992. etc. etc. etc.

A paper prepared for the municipality of Matapédia, by Genivar Groupe (Quebec`s principal hydrology consultant) stated: following clear-cut logging of the Coweeta River Basin, water discharge of threefold increase was recorded, (Swank et al. 1987). Hundreds of studies clearly demonstrate the dramatic increase of spring water yield following deforestation. Not only is water yield increased by removing forest cover, but it also significantly altered the seasonal hydro graph.(Leaf & Brink 1972 etc. etc.)

Timber harvesting causes higher snow-melt rates in early spring, which promotes peaking of the hydro-graph earlier than it would under natural conditions.(Leaf and Alexander 1975)Records for the past one hundred years (next page) clearly indicate that ice runs on the Restigouche River are now happening three weeks earlier than previously.(D`Amours 1994)

Water yields from patch cutting (small clear-cut) can go undiminished for thirty years and longer. Even after this period of time it is conceivable that thirty additional years would be required before runoff increase from initial timber harvest is completely erased.(Leaf and Alexander 1975)Logging roads are the primary cause of erosion.(Rich and Thompson 1971) The treated watershed has considerably more sediment accumulation in the channels from the years immediately following logging operations.(Rich and Thompson 1974)

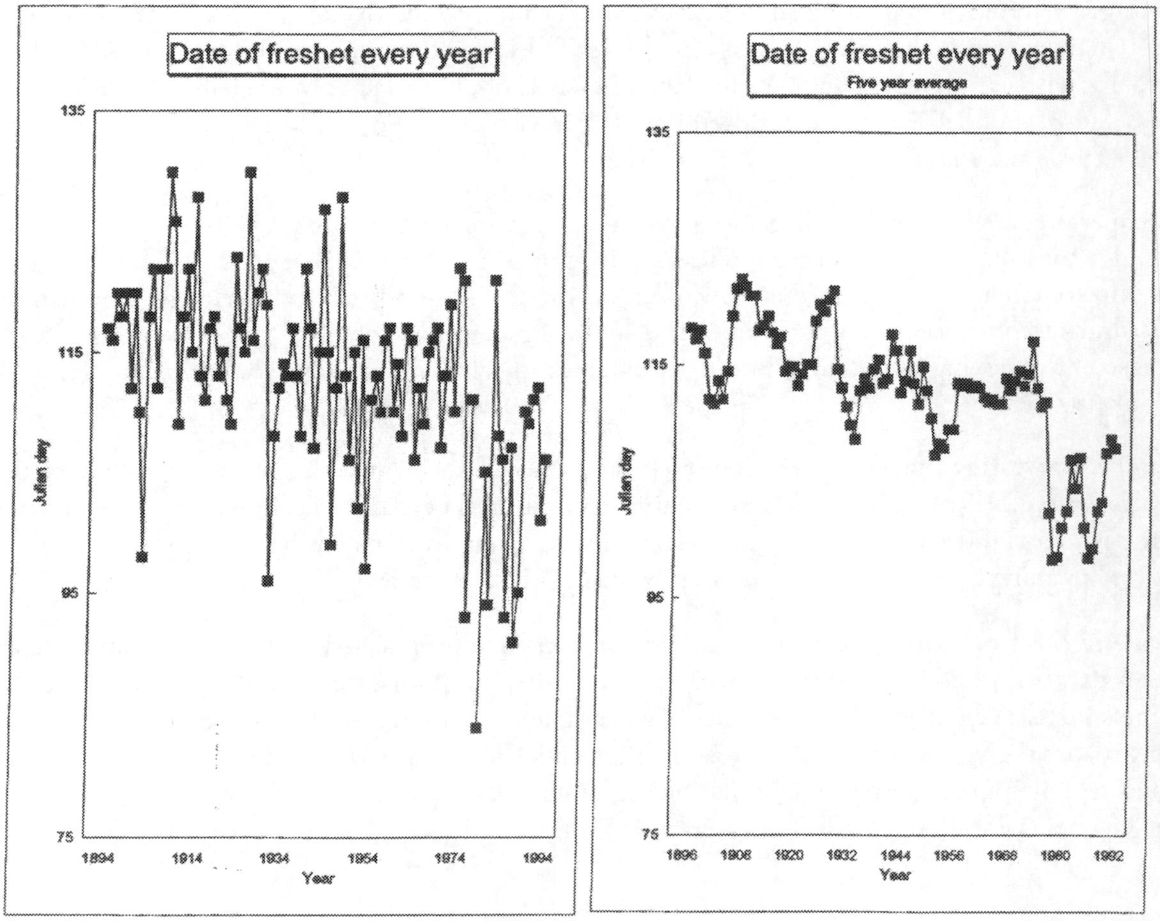

Restigouche river 1894 to 1992

Ice Runs on the Restigouche River are now Occurring Two Weeks Earlier

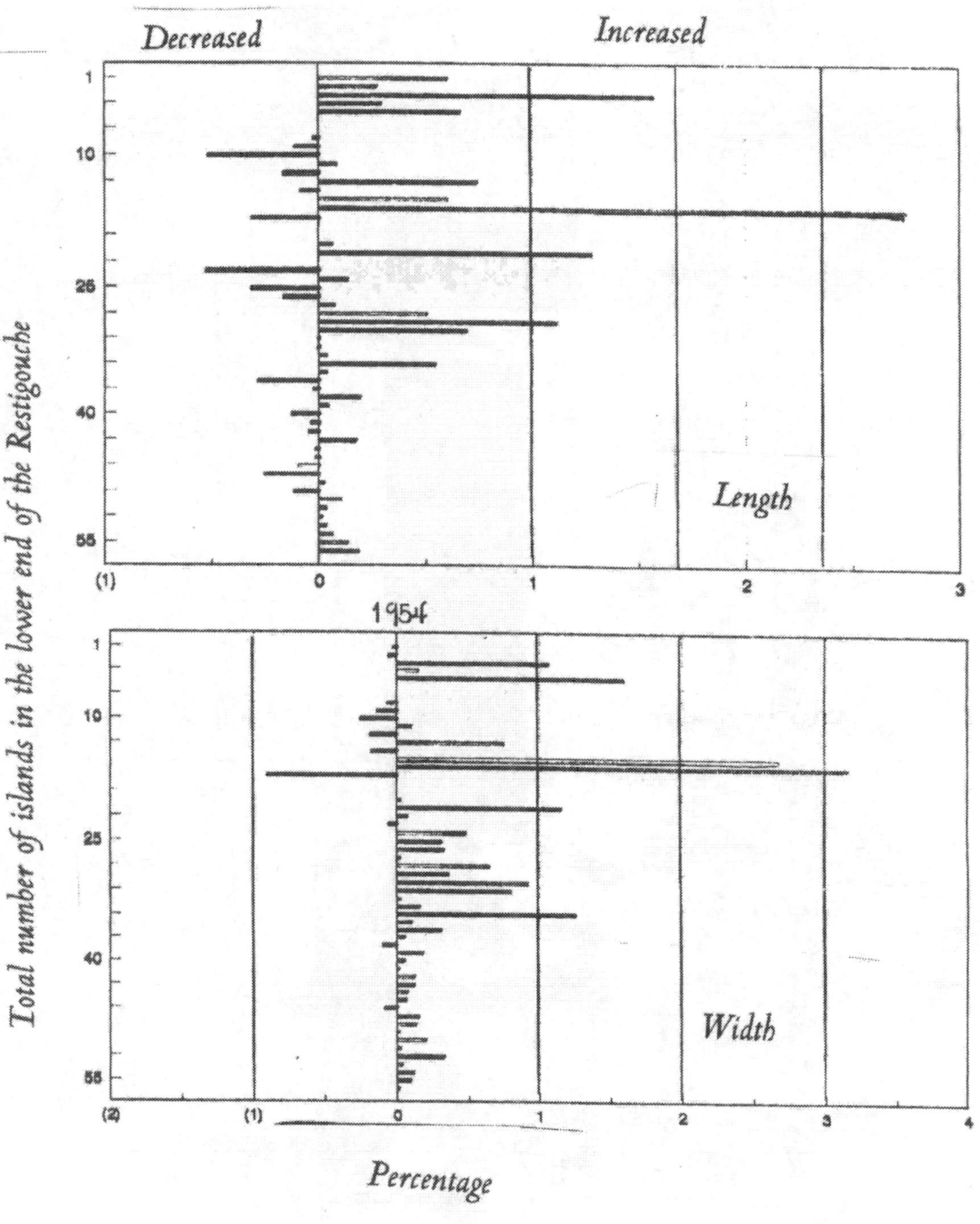

Figure 1. Percentage of variation in length and width of islands in the lower portion of the Restigouche River between 1954 and 1985.

Graph of Islands in Lower Restigouche Showing the Dramatic Increase of Gravel (erosion) Accumulations in the Lower Sector of the River.

Record of important ice flood in Matapédia from 1934 to 1994.

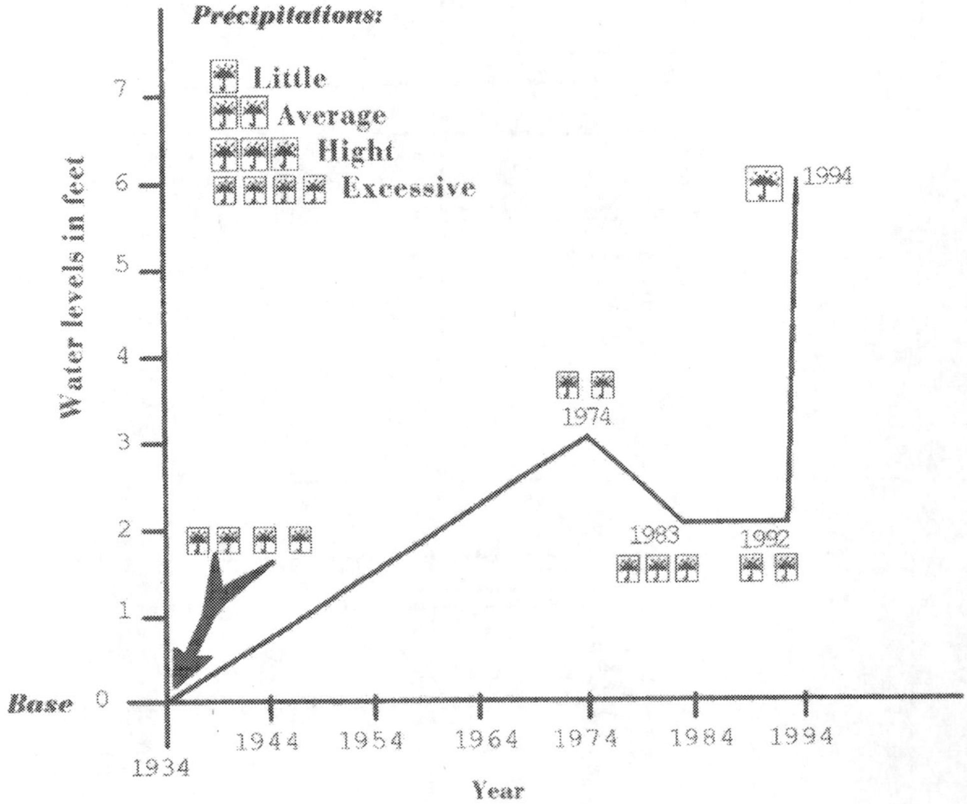

Increase of water levels according to periods

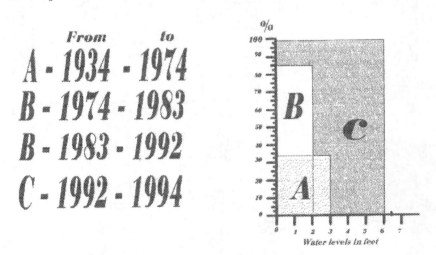

From		to
A - 1934	-	1974
B - 1974	-	1983
B - 1983	-	1992
C - 1992	-	1994

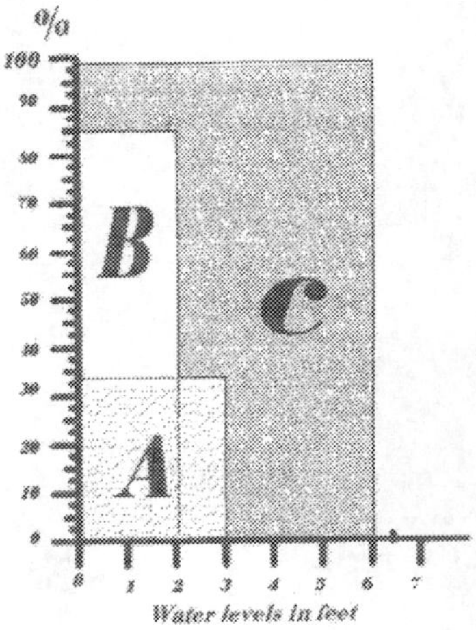

Graph Shows How a Little Rain Can Affect Ice Movements Following Clear-Cut-Logging on the Restigouche River Today

Freezing of the ground is one of the main causes of deterioration of our salmon rivers.(Dubé 1994) As spring arrives, a tremendous amount of water is being produced, by melting snow and possibly accompanied by rain.

In the past, much of this water was absorbed by the land; especially along the Restigouche water shed with the extraordinary capacity of its soil to absorb water.The phenomenally thick topsoil, the Shale (secondary hard layer) which has great water retention properties along with the trees kept water level down to give time for the river ice to wear and melt.This made the ice weak enough to do little damage to the river.It is known that a very large maple tree can drink as much as forty-five gallons of water in one single hot spring day.Also it is known that water, absorbed by the ground, can take over ninety days before reaching the river.Water seeping into the ground delays the ice run in the Restigouche River up to three weeks.

Since the early sixties, clear-cutting practices along the Restigouche River basin have been out of control.

Clear-cutting is still done as of today, right down into brooks and rivers. Good forestry practices are defined by the forestry industry and designed to promote profitability.In truth forestry is as out of control now as it has ever been.The rate and volume of forest removals gives one the impression the industry is urgently trying to cut as much and as quickly as possible.Part of this urgency may be the desire by the forest managers to manage forest species, destroying original species and replanting with commercially desirable species.The objective is to quickly cut down nature's diverse forest and replant it section by section with all one species.These "new forests" are not biologically diverse and do not provide diverse habitats for the various components of the ecosystem.This practice of tree farming disrespects the entire balance of nature.It places private profits ahead of the public interest and violates numerous laws and environmental guidelines prescribed by government.The urgency for the loggers is to cut like crazy before the public realizes what is happening and the urgency for those of us to know what is happening is to sound the alarm and get these abuses halted immediately.

Percentage and frequencies of ice flooding from 1934 to 1994 .

1 ⇨ 1934 - 1974 ***One chance out of forty.***
2,5 % or 1,5 chance

2 ⇨ 1974 -1983 ***One chance out of nine.***
11,1 % or 6,7 chance

3 ⇨ 1983 - 1992 ***One chance out of nine.***
11,1 % or 6,7 chance

4 ⇨ 1992 - 1994 ***One chance out of two.***
50 % or 30 chance

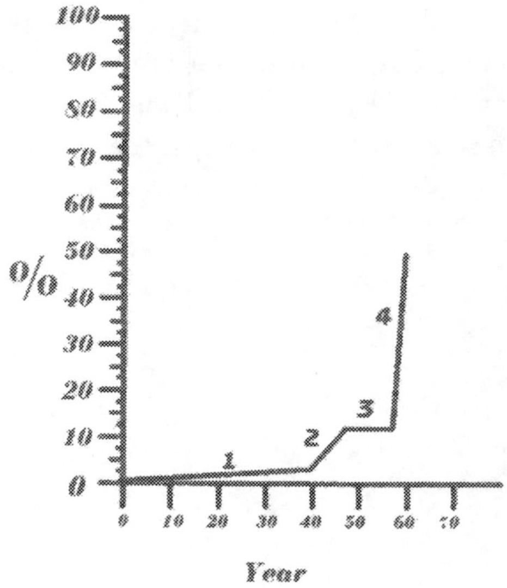

Diagram of comparison

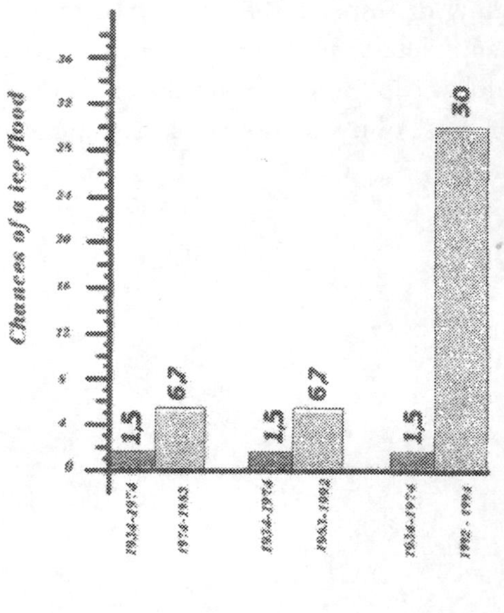

The percentage of a chance of having an ice flood from 1992 - 1994 as compared to 1934 - 1974 has increased by 2000 %

A Ten Thousand Acres Clear-Cut in the Gaspé Peninsula

Thousands of logging roads were built along brooks, gulches and rivers; often smack in the middle of them.Erosion quickly settled in.After heavy rains and spring snow melt, thousands of tons of silt and gravel were dragged along brooks each year, and carried downstream to the main river.I call this phenomenon PRIMARY EROSION.

Up to 1973 the Restigouche flooded perhaps once every forty years. Now there is a major flood every two years; many times more destructive than those of the past.It must be understood that the flooding along the Restigouche River is not to be compared with what is seen frequently on TV.If it were not for the ice dragging the now flat bottom, destroyed channels filled with erosion deposit, and a dramatic 450% increase in spring water yield following totally out of control clear-cut-logging, there would be no ice flooding along the Restigouche River.

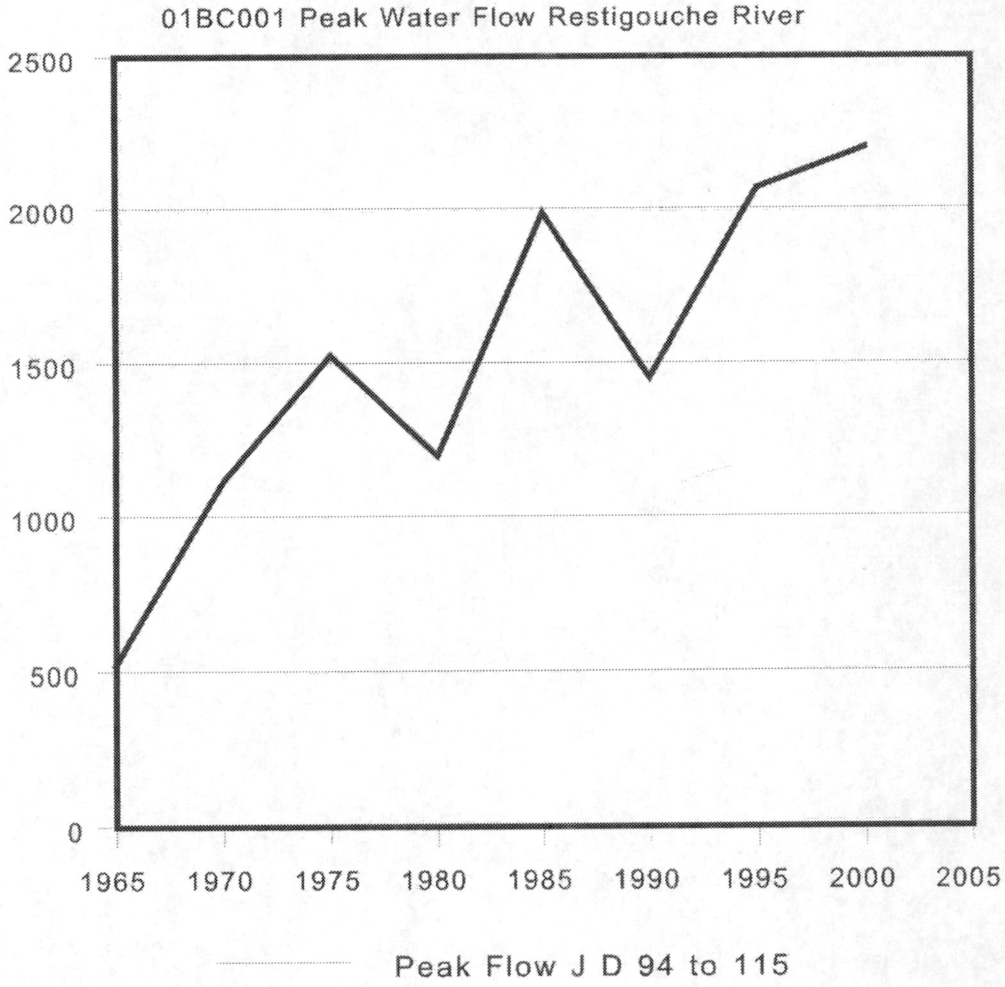

Graph Showing High Water Increase since Totally Out of Control Clear-Cut-Logging Started on the Restigouche River Basin in the early 60's

The highest water level recorded in the Restigouche River, **without ice**, was during the spring of 2008, when it reached about fifteen feet above normal summer level.During the flood of 1994, the level of water **from an ice jam** reached more than thirty feet above normal summer level.This occurred with normal rainfall and a couple of warm days.

Water level at such a height without ice in the Restigouche River is absolutely unthinkable!Can you imagine an ice jam reaching up to thirty-five feet above normal summer level?Imagine the damage done to the bottom and banks of the river!

This was the case here in Matapédia during the spring of 1994.The fall of 1993 was wet; the ground with no protection due to the crushed moss and the lack of trees froze many feet deep. This is just what is needed to create a catastrophic **ice** flood the following spring and the destruction of the riverbed.

<u>And We Had One!..</u>

Let us relive this flood together:

... It `s April the 15th.

... The weather is warm.

... Winter snow accumulation has increased by three folds due to out of control clear-cut-logging, the short rays of the sun in direct contact with the wind transported snow in openings is melting up to three times faster than normal.(As mentioned before in many studies following clear-cut logging)

... Water cannot penetrate the frozen ground in the clear-cutting and on the countless forest roads.

... As recorded by Environment Canada at Hydrology Station 01BC001 the 450% increase in water yield rushes over the frozen surface of the land to the brooks then to the river.

... The ice is still extremely thick and strong.

... The river rises madly.

... The very massive ice is finally pushed into movement weeks earlier than what nature intended.

... Some cakes of ice are ten to twenty times the weight of a large bulldozer.

... Gigantic slabs of extremely thick ice are pushed forward by the torrents of rising water ...- hitting the banks of the river,- tearing them apart,

- transporting the gravel throughout the entire length and width of the river,

- filling in the center of the runs, - filling in the head and tails of salmon pools, - destroying bars, channels and islands.

... Thick ice forces its way through large pools, reshaping them into wide shallow ovals instead of the natural long narrow deeper bowls.

... Occasionally a jam of ice will form, sometime ten to twenty miles in length.

... All water stops circulating; millions of cubic meters of water can accumulates every hour the river is blocked; sometime blocked for days; pressure builds up against the extremely thick ice to the cracking point; a **Giant Tsunami** is formed; backed-up by millions of cubic meters of water; up to twenty miles in length; heading full steam down river like a run-away freight-train.

All this happened in the small village of Matapédia (population 650 residents) on April 17, 1994 causing more than twenty million dollars in damages.

Today, the Restigouche River dumps the bulk of its water in the spring causing a dramatic decreased in summer water flow and the Restigouche River is rapidly becoming as flat as a pan-cake from severe ice runs.The lower two thirds of the river is almost totally ruined, filled in by silt and gravel eroded from far upstream.Today the river is much wider, shallower, has slower currents and the loss of trees along the banks that once offered shade from the sun, have caused an extraordinary increase in water temperature.Water temperature on the Restigouche River during July and August are now reaching the 80 + F.Every biologist knows Atlantic salmon cannot live very long in water this warm.

Note: Global Warming and Climate Change are real issues to be addressed, there is no question about this.The extraordinary temperature changes in the Restigouche River however cannot be explained by Global Warming.We must not accept propaganda from the forest management industry and their environmental spokespeople where they conveniently blame Global Warming for what is absolutely their own responsibility.The temperature rise and the destruction of the river has occurred exactly in the manner and for the reasons we described above.These causes and effects are extremely well documented scientifically and we have cited all necessary studies and provided the evidence.

Ruggedly built Railroad Bridge on lower end of the Restigouche was completely crushed like a weak aluminum beer can, by the massive powerful ice in movement.

St-Alexis Bridge (standing at 24 feet above normal water level) engulfed in ice during the 1994 flood, to be later totally destroyed.(Notice in picture on the right how bridge is bent)

The very massive Interprovincial (CNR) bridge in Matapedia (1400 feet long) during the summer normal water level, its underneath is twenty-seven feet from the surface of the water.Each spring when the Restigouche dumps its ice, the bridge is loaded by the Canadian National Railway with about thirty box cars each fully loaded with rocks weighing some two hundred tons a piece. In 1974 and 1994 the bridge was pushed on its pillars by the massive ice which was moving at some thirty-five feet above normal water level. Imagine the power behind these ice runs on the Restigouche, over the years it has shaved off all the trees bordering its banks.

In clear-cuttings we have lost most of our spring snowmelt water reserve, as it did not penetrate the frozen ground.Now, with no shade to protect it, the ground dries many feet deep.When rains come, it takes a lot of water just to wet the dried soil during normal rainfall, but, in torrential rainfall it runs over the compacted land surface, dragging along millions of tons of sediment.In the virgin forests, the protected ground was not frozen and has accumulated a good water reserve during the spring thaw, with the ground well shaded, and the moss keeping it moist all the time with the nightly dew.Any rainfall keeps water levels up.

Thirty years ago, the Restigouche Salmon Club had a two-ton boat anchored right behind my house.They called it the Mail Boat.Captain Frank Fitzgerald JR. would take up to six 45 gallons drums of gas or diesel fuel, plus grocery for three camps, mail, and other commodities forty-five miles up the Restigouche River from Matapédia every other day. This boat had a 454 cubic inch inboard motor, and had no problem travelling the river in those days.Today we have a hard time getting around during late July and August with a ten horse power motor on a 26 foot canoe, due to destroyed channels and the dramatic decline in summer water flow.

Abusive clear-cutting means that water yield can more than quadruple during spring, and very low water levels in summer, threatening the survival of the Atlantic salmon as temperature rises and oxygen content drops.Disease, such as furunculosis, UDN thrives, and micro-organism multiply in the river like wild fire while sport fishing becomes impossible on many sections of the river.

Land clearing for settlers up river from Matapédia on the Retigouche River was very marginal.It is estimated to be less than two percent of the land surface.All of it was done more than sixty years ago.The sudden changes we have seen on the Restigouche River coincide very precisely with the logging activity.Environment Canada data for meter number 01BC001 located on the Restigouche River, indicated that water flow increased by 450% during Julian day 94 to Julian day 115, from 1963 to 2002. This meter is located where no other activity or modification took place during or after the data recordings. The only activity was totally out of control massive clear-cut-logging operations. It's evident that clear-cut-logging is the only culprit that brought forth this massive erosion problem.Environment Canada data was co-ordinated during the entire recording period including all the factors, thus comparing apples with apples.The equation was calculated with Environment Canada water discharge meter including precipitation data, total rainfall during the period, total winter snow accumulation and air temperature for the period for spring of 1963 to spring of 2002.

There is only one culprit and it is evident!UNCONTROLLED CLEAR-CUT-LOGGING!!!

What I find the most troubling from our government leaders is the fact that they keep on denying that following excessive clear-cut-logging practice dramatic water yield increases occurs. They want to ignore the compound evidence we have shown them.They ignore these studies even as they witness our salmon rivers being torn apart and destroyed by excessive spring water increases. In a letter from the Honourable Frank McKenna then premier of New Brunswick, Mr. McKenna refuses to admit the fact that the Restigouche River water discharges have increased. Premier McKenna writes: "This occurrence is common whether forestry activities have occurred or not. There are more factors, therefore, than forestry operations that caused the unusual flooding of April 1994."He preferred shifting the blame toward an undisclosed reason which in my opinion does not even exist.

In an e-mail from a former client from New Hampshire, who writes of his experience while studying hydrology at the University of New Hampshire where water discharge increases by 500 to 600% were recorded following total clear-cutting of a small water shed.

My client writes: "When I studied hydrology at the University of New Hampshire there was a hillside north of here in the mountains where they completely cut an area and monitored the increase in runoff. I mean they completely cut it, trees, shrubs, anything and everything growing.That showed just what this is showing, 500% to 600% increase in runoff, and it all goes downstream because there is nothing left to hold it".

One has just to go on the Internet and checkout "The Coweeta Experimental Laboratory" or even studies by the University of New Brunswick department of hydrology, all clearly demonstrating without the slightest doubt how clear-cut-logging dramatically increases spring water flows.

It is clear to me our Governments, Federations and Foundations are not taking action to stop the massacre in our forest, and we should be asking ourselves the question . . . Why don't they?

I sent a letter to Mr. Bill Taylor president of the Atlantic Salmon Federation, dated December 1996, letting him know of my concern of what clear-cut-logging was doing to our rivers.Mr Taylor's answer was very polite and courteous, he writes: "I greatly appreciate your keen interest in salmon conservation and the generous support ASF receives from you.I will look into the points raised in your letter and may contact you if I need any further information".

The letter obviously did not bring any changes to the ASF environment protocol, it is business as usual while most salmon rivers on Canada's East Coast and the United States are being destroyed by out of control clear-cut-logging.

For nearly a half a century, I have been exposed to just about every aspect and circumstance that one can experience in the world of Atlantic salmon.The countless hours of fishing, the endless discussions with anglers from around the world, the opportunity of having fished with some of the most informed and dedicated fly fishermen, many of whom earned their living in the salmon industry.I have also hunted for over twenty-five consecutive years with friends who are large logging operators.One cannot help but to learn a lot from these professional woodcutters.

The report I have written here on the effects of clear-cut logging, the devastating massacre carried out by the log drive and the countless dams that were built in most of our river tributaries to perform the drive, the massive erosion effects.These facts are backed by dozens of scientific studies and actual recordings of these events taking place in which one can see on videotape up to five bulldozers at a time all working together on a pulp drive in the main Kedgewick River, and most tributaries of the Restigouche River.On the same tape one can see dynamite explosions in the Restigouche River propelling logs hundreds of feet into the air. The legendary Richard Nelson Adams was Forman on most of those jobs, at one time having over six hundred men working under his command. Mr. Adams played a major role in the destruction of the Restigouche River Basin during these log drives operations, which he very regretfully admitted in the later years of his life.

The Restigouche River has aged much much faster than nature intended due to clear-cut-logging. The resulting effects, in the form of a tremendous increase of spring water yield following deforestation, is the real **culprit** that is devastating our salmon rivers. This early dramatic increase in early spring water yield provokes this **massive ice to movement prematurely**, tearing the river to shreds, thus causing what I have named . . . **<u>SECONDARY EROSION</u>.**

You will find on the next few pages diagrams showing how erosion affects your favourite salmon pool and what it does to the fishing. The first diagram is a **TOP** view and shows how ice can dig at the banks of the river making it much wider, sending this gravel to the centre of the river, slowly filling in the channel, thus making the river shallower

A salmon pool before erosion

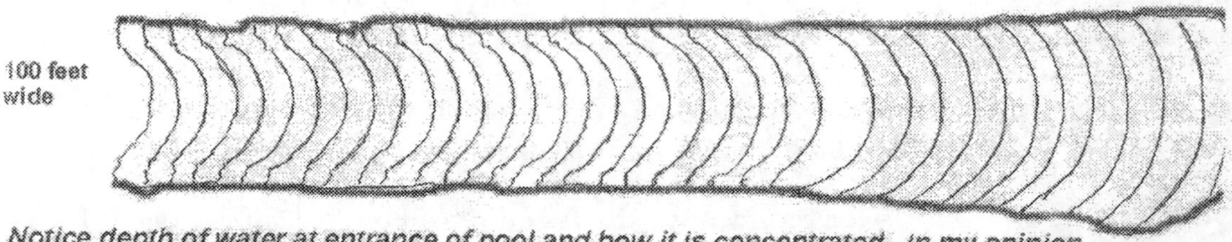

Notice depth of water at entrance of pool and how it is concentrated. In my opinion our rivers have widened by some 25% just in the last thirty years. The water temperature change very little when water has depth and less surface in contact with the elements.

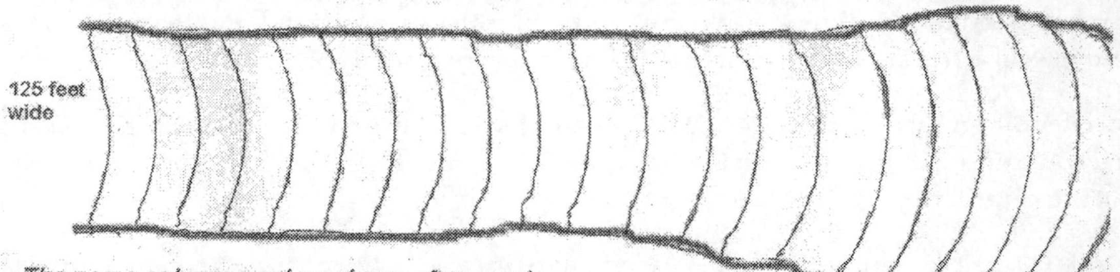

The same salmon pool as above after erosion.
Shallowness and width are the result of mostly secondary erosion caused by very thick ice pushed into movement some three weeks earlier than what nature intended. Shallowness and width will cause erratic water temperature, putting the fish down, thus spoiling the fishing.

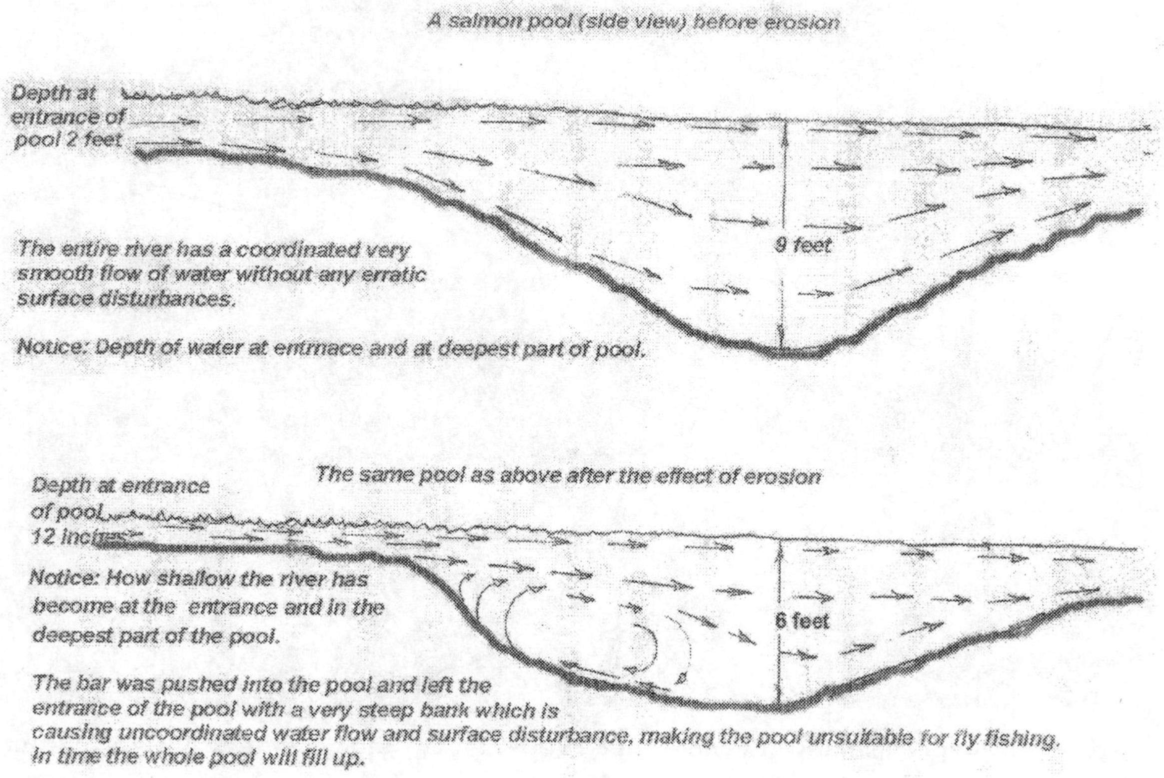
A salmon pool (side view) before erosion
Depth at entrance of pool 2 feet
9 feet
The entire river has a coordinated very smooth flow of water without any erratic surface disturbances.
Notice: Depth of water at entrnace and at deepest part of pool.
The same pool as above after the effect of erosion
Depth at entrance of pool 12 inc
Notice: How shallow the river has become at the entrance and in the deepest part of the pool.
6 feet
The bar was pushed into the pool and left the entrance of the pool with a very steep bank which is causing uncoordinated water flow and surface disturbance, making the pool unsuitable for fly fishing. In time the whole pool will fill up.

This Graph Shows the Damage done to our Rivers by Ice Flooding

There is no question that the Restigouche River is a very long way from what it used to be.

Meeting of Matapedia and Restigouche June 1950 (Notice canoe in middle of river in front of house)

Meeting of Matapedia and Restigouche in May 1994

Today in front of that same house where the canoe was anchored, is an island 1500 feet long by 250 wide and about 9 feet high.

The diagram on previous pages shows what gigantic slabs of very thick ice in movement can do to your favourite salmon pool.This ice performs like a bulldozer pushing gravel into the pool leaving the head of it with a very steep bank initially and causes erratic water flow. Eventually this steep erosion bank will creep throughout the entire pool until it is completely filed.

The decrease of water during the summer months is absolutely devastating to the salmon and the angler, as water temperature can change two to three time faster in just one day as it did in the same period just thirty years ago.

Add to this the real effect of global warming, (I will give you more information on global warming later) with increased UV rays which are stronger today, and compounding it to our now deteriorated salmon habitat and you can bet trouble is just around the corner.

All together these conditions have made it impossible for salmon to find the proper protection from the sun, except in a few very deep sections and the very top headwaters of our salmon rivers.

This protection was available in the past due to the cover of deep rapids with surface waves that deflected sun light, and the shadow created by trees that once bordered our rivers banks.One can easily imagine the stress the eyes of salmon are subjected to by direct sunlight during the entire summer with no eyelids or sunglasses for protection.No wonder salmon don't take a fly as well as they used to!

Just forty some years ago where the water line on most salmon rivers meet the beach, trees slanted toward the river at about a forty-five degree angle and often on both sides of the river. These trees covered the beaches and most importantly shaded the water surface, today it's mostly all gone.

This changed environment makes it practically impossible for salmon to look up toward the sky on bright sunny days; thus, most likely they will not detect the angler's fly cruising by.

Salmon just don`t feel secure any more in this deteriorated environment due to the loss of natural cover.

Today, accomplished anglers have learned the importance of fly presentation in relation to the direction of sunlight.Before the mid-seventies, salmon were just as eager to take a fly on sunny days as well as on overcast ones, except maybe during very low water conditions.

The modern angler will need to earn his/her fishing success by planning wisely his/her angling strategies.Paying very close attention to sunlight direction, variation between air and water temperature, including speed of flow, time of day when sunlight gets on or off pools, all these are a must for regular success.

In Reverend Rigginy`s book, ´´ Salmon Taking Time `` his theory is that salmon do not take a fly if air temperature is colder than that of the water temperature.I have to agree with his theory in general.Naturally there are possibly exceptions to this rule, but not very often.

Here is an illustration of how you should plan your next evening fishing during late August when the phenomena of air temperature being colder than that of water is very frequent.

Remember! . . Two important elements need to be considered . . . The difference between air temperature versus water temperature, plus the intensity, the direction and timing of sun light ON and OFF the pool.

To dramatically increase your chance if success, choose a good salmon pool, not necessarily the one with the best known reputation for success, in this case select the one with the best flow of water and with the earliest evening sunlight OFF its surface.It is preferable not to fish the pool you have chosen until sunlight is OFF of it. The minute the sun gets OFF . . . if it's a long pool on a big river, concentrate only on fishing the hot spot, (the honey hole) so you can cover a possibly taking salmon before the cold evening air of August rushes in and becomes colder than the temperature of the water.The above method is Rigginy`s salmon taking time theory.

Water temperature in late August is usually warm and the evening air gets cold very quickly as the sun goes down over the mountain.Thus the salmon taking time is short, and anglers should use the above Rigginy technique to improve their catch.

From now on pay closer attention to pool angle in relation to the sunlight direction during the day.

On the Matapedia River the famous Salmon Hole Pool is a typical example of what I call a good MORNING pool to fish, as the sunlight direction is on the tail of the salmon.But this pool does not have much to offer on bright sunny evenings (even if the pool is full of fish) as the bright sunlight stays directly in the salmon's eyes until just before darkness arrives.However, once dusk settles in on Salmon Hole . . . GO AT IT! . .Especially if the air temperature is warmer than that of the water it should be a winning situation.To improve angling success salmon fishermen will have to pay extra attention to sunlight direction as our salmon habitat keeps deteriorating.

During the seventies, following the lifting of the commercial nets in the Bay des Chaleurs, salmon fishing was just absolutely awesome!

The sweetest memories from my entire salmon angling experience, happened during these exceptional angling years.I can clearly remember when my faithful friend Guy Moores (Veteran guide extraordinaire of the RSC) restlessly stuck around the Hotel as late May arrived.Guy's years of fishing experience and his well-bred natural instinct . . . just knew if a fresh run of GIANT salmon had entered the river.Not much coaxing was required on his part to convince me we should be heading up river.During our discussions and planning for our voyage on the Patapédia, we never . . . I MEAN NEVER! Talked about the possibility of not catching salmon!That thought never crossed our minds.

A three hours' catch on the Ristigouche (one rod)

In the Good Old Days One Rod Three Hours of Fishing

In those days before we converted to the catch and release philosophy, what preoccupied us the most was how we were going to take them back!

An early June catch during the mid-seventies on the Patapédia River could regularly produce the daily limit of four salmon per day for two anglers, and often all fish weighed over thirty pounds.

Deforestation can under certain conditions yield temporary benefits to salmon. In fact it can increase the amount of fish spawning, as the sport fishery is catching fewer salmon, due to lower and warmer water levels and a deteriorated habitat. Thus, more fish are left in the river to spawn. That might sound like good news for conservationists to boast about for now! . .Government and Salmon River administrators have capitalised on that reality for boosting their image . . . but, this phenomenon will not keep on playing in their favour for much longer!

This phenomenon of salmon swimming through to the headwaters has prompted the administrators of many salmon rivers to open up the once sanctuaries in the head waters of these rivers to anglers, thus putting even more pressure on our salmon stocks. This is especially true for the early runners, which are our most valuable strain of fish, thus increasing their vulnerability. Salmon rivers administrators and governments have extended the salmon season on most of our rivers, from a three months season on the Restigouche River to a five and a half months season today. The salmon establishment is desperately trying to cover up the dramatic reduction of season licenses now sold by offering day pass, three days pass, season catch and release at $10.25 as to increase the bottom line for licenses sold and sales still continue to decline.

The deterioration of our rivers and the effect it has on migration and salmon survival as I have mentioned before, has increased considerably more rapidly than I had anticipated.

On the Restigouche River we frequently hear blame placed on the large traffic of canoeist for the phenomenon of salmon travelling straight up to the headwaters.This is far from accurate as we see the same problem on other rivers that don't have the canoeists.It is not to be said that canoeists have no effect on salmon fishing.No doubt they don't help the anglers to catch salmon.

It is evident that there are now less salmon that spawn in the main river and most eggs don't survive the ravaging consequences of accumulated slush in that portion of the river when it freezes in the late fall.

The river being wider, shallower and slower in summer months, has in the fall the reverse temperature effects.It now cools down too quickly sending the colder water slush to the bottom, and the warmer water on the bottom is exchanged, and rises to the surface.

The picture below shows slush sticking to the bottom of the river directly over salmon spawning beds before the river freezes.This increasing phenomenon of slush sticking to the bottom is caused by surface water molecules cooling down too rapidly, creating an exchange where hotter water at the bottom rises to the surface, while the colder slush on top is forced underneath by the logic of gravity.

Slush Sticking to Bottom of River on Salmon Spawning Ground

It's well documented that salmon are like pigeons and return to the very same spot in which they were born.Thus, it's in the tributaries and not in the main river that salmon eggs survive best.This is due to less slush accumulation as water molecules in the headwaters are exposed for only a short period of time to the cold air, and in a less destroyed environment for the present.Meanwhile in the main river, slush can pile up ten to twenty feet high, like lava flowing down a volcano, killing most salmon eggs.

This explains why we see salmon in June and early July travel straight up to the headwaters of our rivers, too busy to take a fly, leaving only the odd stragglers in the lower end of the river.

Slush Creeping Downriver like Lava Flowing from a Volcano

As this phenomenon of habitat deterioration accelerates and rapidly creeps to the upper end of our tributaries, the truth will then come to the surface, as evidence will no longer be possible to hide. The administrators of our salmon rivers will then be bathing in embarrassment for having misled anglers and hidden the truth from them for years.

Following Clear-cut logging, the lack of trees intercepting snow can increase total winter snow accumulations on the ground by as much as three folds or more.Exterminating the effect of evapo-sublimation (Snow evaporating on contact of sunrays on trees, and dispersed in the atmosphere in a gaseous state) by clear-cut logging can more than quadruple spring water yield!This increase of spring water yield will prematurely provoke ice movement, thus initiating ice flooding, destroying the river, spoiling salmon habitat and the quality of angling.

In virgin forests snow on trees will vaporize in the atmosphere, leaving a third of the winter snow accumulations on the ground or even less.

Evaposublimation at Work in the Gaspé Park

The more abundant and the larger the clear-cuts, the more abundant and the more powerful winds become.(Wind speed at ground level is two point five time faster in clear-cut openings, in contrast to wind speed at ground level in forest cover.Cline, Haupt, and Campbell, June 1977.)

In large clear-cut openings, winds will pick-up momentum that can generate dramatic velocity increases.This increased wind speed crashes into unprotected forest cover, knocking down countless matured trees.

These broken trees, known as '' **Blow-Downs**`` are then pointed out by the logging companies as ... '' **See ... matured forests have to be cut, it will just rot there if not logged!**`` **Naturally,** the logging companies are not admitting that clear-cutting is a **major** cause of blow-downs.

The Matapedia Valley CANADIAN FORESTRY CAPITAL ...

Let's Stand on Guard for Thee . . .

Chapter Two

The Salmon Establishment and Business as Usual . . .

Following the introduction of my first paper, in December of 1996 on the effects of uncontrolled clear-cut logging and river pulp log drive, I have become even more concerned, due mainly to the lack of response shown by our federations and individuals responsible for the protection of our salmon rivers.

When I did not receive any response at all from the FQSA (Fédération Québecoise pour le Saumon Atlantique) and only a short "brush-off" letter from Bill Taylor, president of the ASF, (Atlantic Salmon Federation) I knew then that something was very wrong.

The ASF is the most powerful Atlantic salmon conservation organization we have on the East Coast and most of its members depend entirely upon the directors and executive officers of that organization to do what is necessary to protect our salmon and their habitat.Until now, no one has questioned if this is really the case!Subsequently, it has become very clear that we have left the hen house open for the fox to enter as it pleases.Should the thousands of members of the ASF and FQSA take for granted that their favourite conservation organizations are doing all they can to save salmon and its habitat?We will explore this question in more detail and the readers may form their own conclusions.

Shouldn't we investigate whether any possible conflicts of interest exist within our so called "conservation" organizations that may be intimidating the proper administration of their mission?If so, could this result in them making decisions which could even be detrimental to our salmon and rivers?

Therefore, can we not scrutinize more closely the leaders in the front row and behind the scene of these organizations regarding their relationships with big industries?Can we observe by their actions, where their true loyalties are?

In my opinion we have a lot to be concerned about . . . I recommend that all anglers interested in the well being of our salmon and its habitat start paying **very close** attention to what is going on within our salmon conservation organizations.Do not be reticent in questioning our federations representatives.You will find that persistence is required to get clear straightforward answers and you will also find that things are not always as they appear.Getting the truth in these matters is a lot like fishing because its what's going on "beneath the surface" that really counts.

In my opinion, our Federations in Eastern Canada are controlled by the logging industry and the wealthy riparian owners, also by a select group of influential individuals (some of whom hold, or have had held, positions of authority in government). It is clear to me, and extensive inquiry into this matter only serves to solidify this conviction, that these individuals and the giant paper and logging interests they serve, are the orchestrators and primary beneficiaries of many of the most important programs and policies that issue from these Federations. Many of their most critical decisions do not serve to benefit either the public or the Atlantic Salmon but **only to benefit the riparian owners and to deflect attention from the catastrophic environmental destruction perpetrated by the forest industry which was described earlier.** If this continues, these Federations will never adopt the policies and promote the measures that are required to save our salmon and they will most certainly continue to vigorously protect the private fishing rights of the riparian owners.Who is working for the rights of the rest of us ordinary salmon anglers?Should we even mention again the rights of Atlantic salmon to survive as a wild species?

During February of 1998, on Radio Canada National Television News the following was announced: The Federal Government will have to intervene in matters of pollution control within the Province of Quebec, as some paper companies have defaulted many times the pollution control regulations and no charges have been laid.Among these companies, The Roland Paper Co. was cited as having defaulted many times, Mr. Lucien Roland is the owner of the Roland Paper Company and he was also chairman of the Board of the Atlantic Salmon Federation.

On September 10, 1970, CBC announces, "Irving Whale goes down" with 4200 tons of heavy "C" bunker oil and 7.2 tons of PCB's in the Gulf of St-Laurence.Even though reports indicate that the Irving Whale was swamped due to negligence, the Irving family refuses responsibility and the Whale Tanker is still as of today (1995) leaking its oil and PCB's in the Gulf of St-Laurence. Why in the world has the Canadian government permitted Irving to get away with leaving the Irving Whale with its remaining cargo at the bottom of the ocean, knowing very well that it would eventually leak all of its content in the Gulf of St-Laurence?Still as of 2008 commercial fishermen are not allowed to harvest any species from the area where the Whale went down due to the high concentration of PCB's in that area. This is one of the most horrendous environmental crime in Canada's history and responsibility for this event remains unaccounted for.We will come back to the Irving Whale later.

Mr. Lucien Rolland and Mr. J. D. Irving are two major pillars of the Atlantic Salmon Federation.

At a special meeting (after the 1994 flood) of the Matapédia Municipal Council concerning the causes and prevention of ice flooding within the village of Matapédia, the Genivar Group, one of Quebec's most respected firms in matters of river management was invited by the municipality to attend.

Also present, were the mayor along with municipal councillors, and half dozen interested citizens including myself.Claude Beaulieu and André St-Hilaire were representing the Genivar Group, a consultant firm in salmon biology, river restoration and hydrology management. Most hydroelectric project and Salmon River restorations in Quebec are often made under the supervision of Genivar Group.Mr. Gilles Shooner is one of the main administrators and he is also very much involved with the Quebec Salmon Federation.Mr. Shooner is very well aware of the extreme impact clear-cut-logging is having on our salmon rivers.I have made sure to accurately inform Mr. Schooner of the devastation that past and current forestry practices are having on our salmon rivers, unfortunately without results.

The purpose of the meeting was to find a solution to the rapidly deteriorating morphology of the Restigouche River system, mainly the accumulation of gravel bars at the lower end of the river which are causing major ice flooding problems for the village of Matapédia.

Notice how gravel bars accumulated in center of river at junction of Matapédia and Restigouche

At a point during this meeting, I asked Mr. St-Hilaire, and Mr. Beaulieu . . ."Considering that the ice movement on the Restigouche River presently occurs some three weeks earlier than was the case just forty years ago; considering that it is recognized and well documented that river volume does increase considerably with the intensity of clear-cut logging; should it not be easy to demonstrate, that clear-cut logging and its massive erosion effects are the cause of the constantly increasing intensity, and frequency, of major ice flooding on the Restigouche River"?

Their answer:''Yes in theory this is true, but, since there was no monitoring of water discharge taken on the Restigouche River prior to 1972, your evaluation is just simply theory and impossible to prove``. I asked: ''Are you absolutely sure that there are no records of water discharge on the Restigouche prior to 1972, because I do not believe you . . . They must have recorded the river discharge volumes before 1972.Is it possible that you do not have any records of that? ``

Their answer: '' We guarantee you that no records whatsoever exist of water discharge for the Restigouche River system prior to 1972.Hydrology is our specialty and we can guarantee you that if any records whatsoever existed for the Restigouche River prior to 1972 we would be the people who would know about it. ``

This discussion proceeded until I knew there was no way our two hydrology experts could back down on their position.This I wanted to make sure of, as I knew they were lying. I then made my presentation with charts showing water discharge taken on the Upsulquich River (tributary of the Restigouche River) since 1920.

When I brought these charts to the table for everyone to see, we suddenly had two very nervous and pale faced hydrologists stuttering . . . ´´ Where did you get this? ! ! ! ``

You will find a graph below of water discharge for the Upsulquich River (1920 compared to 1991) plus a condensed chart on the following pages of the Restigouche River from spring of 1963 to spring of 2002.

The condensed chart information was taken from Environment Canada published data for meter number 01BC001, located on the Restigouche just below the Kedgwick River.There is also a second meter on the Restigouche River 01BJ007 located just above the Rafting Ground.Meter 01BJ007 was installed in 1968 and reveals similar results for the

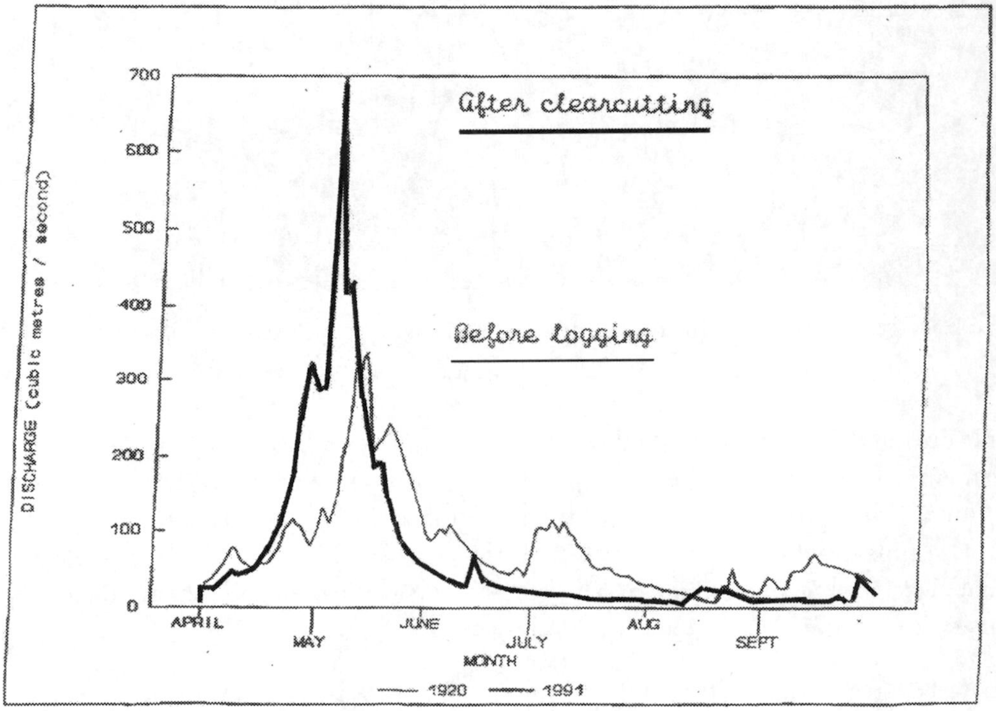

Upsalquitch River

same period.After observing the data from Environment Canada I have found that peak **low** water flows at meter number 01BC001 have increased during the same period by a shocking 1592%, (on next page) that is 15.92 time what it was in 1963.And also when taking in both cases the highest peak flows out of the equation from the first five year average and the last five year average the water yield increases to an astonishing 624%

One of the earliest lessons in modern physics was developed by Daniel Bernoulli about 300 years ago.Bernoulli's Principal regarding the dynamics of the movement of fluids shows that increasing volume and velocity increases pressure.Pressure is force.One does not have to be a plumber to understand that a four and one half inch water pipe running at full capacity, cannot be made to pass through a one inch pipe without things bursting apart from everywhere. That's exactly what is happening to our salmon rivers when totally out of control clear-cut-logging is performed on a watershed.

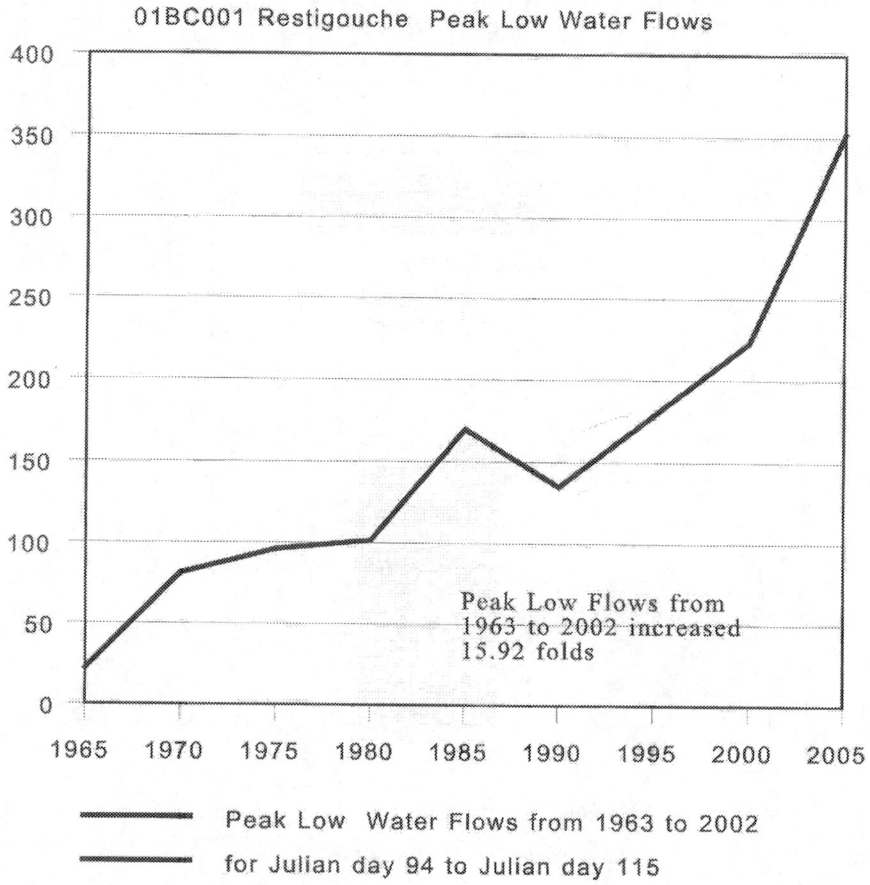

Now, I ask you, the readers, who is covering up this evidence of environmental destruction?Who benefits from the profits of illegal logging practices?Who is responsible for regulating the logging industry?Use your own common sense!This situation is utterly outrageous!There is obviously too much coziness between the government regulators and the logging industry they regulate.We must also deal with this same insidious "coziness" between our Federations and the logging industry which is extremely dangerous due to the potential for manipulating the "science" and the studies they produce.

The leadership of the Atlantic Salmon Federation as well as the Quebec Salmon Federation knew very well what is going on and we will continue to visit this subject in later chapters.

How to read the chart on the next two pages:

First row: The year (From the 94th day of the year to the 115th day)
Second row: Highest daily peak water flow recorded during the period
Third row: Highest daily peak water flow total for the entire period
Fourth row: Average daily temperature for the period
Fifth row: Rain in Kedgwick for the period
Sixth row: Winter snow accumulation
Seventh row: Rain in Edmonston for the period

O1BC001 Year	Peak Flow	Julian day 94 to 115	Average Temp	Rain Kedgwick	Winter Snow	Rain Edmonst
1963	58.3	469.	2.4	49.5	362.	49.5
1964	110.	617.	2.6	25.9	335.	29.0
1965	69.9	682.	2.8	18.0	278.	24.9
1966	261.	2218.	3.3	14.0	326.	11.9
1967	22.1	343.	1.1	5.1	289.	18.0
Total:	521.3	4329.	2.44	A22.5	A318.	A26.7
1968	481.	4967.	4.8	53.8	325.	76.5
1969	251.	1720.	0.9	11.2	402.	33.3
1970	156.	1055.	2.6	24.4	283.	39.9
1971	147.	1342.	2.6	35.3	411.	46.0
1972	81.3	795.	0.7	3.3	471.	15.5
Total:	1116.	9879.	2.32	A25.6	A378.	A42.2
1973	484.	2946.	3.1	79.5	415.	106.9
1974	96.3	1175.	1.4	57.4	374.	68.8
1975	130.	1044.	0.9		350.	22.6
1976	345.	4521.	2.5	107.4	460.	107.4
1977	473.	2602.	1.8	9.4	436.	32.1
Total:	1528.	12288	1.94	A55.3	A407	A67.6
1978	102.	669.	1.8	20.6	419.	35.1
1979	212.	2501.	3.9	61.0	300*	73.3
1980	376.	3098.	4.8	36.4	300*	67.0
1981	381.	4458.	3.6	72.2	242.	82.0
1982	126.	1056.	2.8	30.9	261.	37.0
Total:	1197.	11782	3.38	A44.2	A304.	A58.9

01BC001 Year	Peak Flow	Julian day 94 to 115	Average Temp	Rain Edmonst	Winter Snow	Rain Kedgwick
1983	620.	5225.	4.0	70.1	300*	117.0
1984	346.	3442.	4.1	27.3	250.	31.2
1985	170.	1181.	0.6	24.0	189.	37.8
1986	465.	4340.	5.5	26.8	284.	56.8
1987	384.	4611.	4.6	19.9	160.	33.0
Total:	1985.	18798	3.76	A33.6	A237.	A55.2
1988	250.	4575.	3.6	56.0	286.	
1989	135.	2193.	2.5	44.8	294.	
1990	277.	2543.	3.6	47.4	274.	32.0
1991	411.	2807.	3.0	45.4	256.	24.2
1992	377.	1856.	2.1	59.6	184.	40.6
Total:	1450.	13974	2.96	A50.6	A259.	N/A
1993	597.	5486.	3.8	76.5	227.	78.4
1994	420.	3208.	2.0	80.7	286.	60.1
1995	310.	2006.	0.9	35.9	266.	
1996	519.	2472.	3.4	84.3	184.	
1997	223.	779.	3.0	16.3	393.	
Total:	2069.	13952	2.62	A58.7	A271.	N/A
1998	458.	5254.	3.5	37.0	259.	
1999	352.	3435.	3.1	7.1	216.	
2000	590.	5485.	2.3	70.5	270.	
2001	381.	1046.	2.9	13.0	300*	
2002	435.	4037	3.2	32.0	288.	
Total:	2216.	19257	3.00	A31.9	A267.	N/A

Raping the Environment and Attempted Murder!

A well documented event during the Indian Fishery crisis of 1976 demonstrates extraordinarily underhanded and ruthless behaviour bordering on criminal intent.It shows that the underlings of the Riparian Rights owners, who are running our Federations, will go to any length to protect their master's private fishing interests:

At a meeting during the Indian fishery crisis (at the mouth of the Restigouche River) in the late summer of 1976, were present, Wilfred Carter, president of the ASF, André Vézina, president of the FQSA, with Charles Langlois director, and our association SORMER, (Société d`Opération des Rivières Matapédia et Restigouche) represented by me as president, plus a few of our directors. This meeting was to finalize the project which involved two men who were hired by the SORMER to monitor the salmon count on the Restigouche River which was being netted by the Listuguj Indian Reserve 12 miles downstream from Matapédia.

The project was financed half by the ASF, and the balance equally shared by the FQSA and the SORMER.

The conclusion of this project "Observation Count of the Aboriginal Fishery on the Restigouche River", indicated clearly that the Indian fishery quota was not respected and was easily exceeded by some tenfold.It had always been, and still remains, my position that matters involving like this involving Aboriginal rights, must be discussed with the Tribal Councils of Elders as a first step, rather than provoking the confrontations that have failed so miserably in the past.

At a point during this meeting Wilfred Carter addressed me and said ´´ Pete, we have all the necessary evidence required to bring the Indians of Listuguj to court for exceeding their quota, and not respecting the signed agreement.The ASF will pay for the best lawyers and will absorb all expenses involved if you lay charges against the Indians of Listuguj and bring them before a judge?"As the evidence was strong and revealed a truly alarming amount of damage to the fishery, I agreed with his position.

My answer to Wilfred Carter was ´´ No problem so long as one representative from each club on the entire Restigouche River joins me". Mister Carter answered: ´´ Oh NO!We cannot do that! `` I asked ´´ why not? `` He answered:´´ If we do that the Indians might come upriver to burn **<u>OUR CAMPS</u>**, so; it is out of the question for **<u>us</u>** to get **<u>our</u>** clubs involved! `` (It is interesting that the president of the Atlantic Salmon Federation refers to the camps, which are owned by the who's who of North American billionaires, as "our camps".)In any event, I answered . . . ´´Wilf! I don't even own one inch of water on the Restigouche and have a Hotel establishment worth many times any of the club houses on the entire Restigouche River Basin, and you expect me to take the Indians to court alone?It's out of the question! `` Wilfred Carter, returned to the comfort of his St-Andrews office, while I kept struggling through government channels for a ban on these netting practice.

Almost right away I began receiving threats on my life and I was even warned by my niece Tammy Fitzgerald who was dating a MicMac Indian from the Listuguj Reserve that there were rumours of a pending Indian attack on me at my place of business.At a private meeting with the local Chief of Police Mr. Jacques Létourneau and the Mayor Mr. Jean Poirier, I was advised to take whatever steps were necessary to defend myself and protect my property.Early one evening, seven months after our joint directors meetings with Wilfred Carter, an angry mob of around two dozen Indians attacked my place of business and caused many thousands of dollars of damage.I will always remember the sound of breaking glass as maybe a half dozen men smashed through my front door with axes, screaming and yelling as they came for me with axes and crowbars.It all happened so fast that for a moment I could not even believe this was happening.It was over just as fast.During this struggle to save my life and my business, I had to shoot four Indians with a twelve-gauge shotgun.I am very, very, lucky to be alive, and also lucky to have been prepared for the worst.I am no gun toting Rambo and I am against using deadly force on human beings.That is why, in planning for my own defence, my gun was loaded with bird shots, and not buck shot or slugs. Fortunately no one was killed in this modern day "Battle of the Restigouche" and for this I am very thankful.

Following this attack I contacted my Uncle the Honourable Jean Eudes Dubé who had just stepped down as Minister of Public Works for Canada and was then Judge of the Federal Court. I needed to have a legal and or a political solution to resolve this incident and to prevent more violence. Luckily Uncle Jean Eudes Dubé was a very close friend to the Honourable Warren Almond who was Minister of Indian Affairs, although as a judge Uncle Jean Eudes could not comment but I was hopeful it could be helpful for him to be informed.

I was advised to bring charges against twenty-two individuals who participated in the assault.At the first court hearing, I was taken aside by the Crown Prosecutor and a lawyer and was told, ''If you drop the charges against these twenty-two Indians, we will guarantee you full protection, so that these individuals will no longer harass you in any way, shape or form . . . And if not, then we cannot guarantee anything". So, common sense indicated I should drop the charges; thus being left to absorb the entire bill of repair without any compensation.I have no doubt that if this case were to have proceeded to trial we would have learned exactly who were the real provocateurs of the attack.As it is now we are left with only rumours and suspicions.At this stage in life I hold no grudge in the matter and have since trained numerous Indians from the reserve to be professional fishing guides, an occupation that they are good at and highly qualified by heritage and life-style to perform.

Who would have thought back then that Wilfred Carter, would not even show the slightest sign of support following this assault against my life after we worked so closely together on the Indian Fishery problems and especially since he was so vocal about having me initiate strong measures to confront the Indians in the first place.I have always wondered if he or his "buddies" at the clubs may have actually provoked the Indians to focus their anger and resentments on me personally rather than to be man enough to take a stand publicly and show a little personal courage in this difficult matter. None the less, Wilfred Carter and his "Federation" were quick to take all the credit for the eventual success of reducing the Indian nets and the marginal improvements in salmon returns that resulted as we will see later.

The relationship between the Aboriginal Peoples and Atlantic salmon is a very special one which must be respected.We are all learning how to work together to honour their heritage and to guarantee the Aboriginals' rights to harvest salmon.But there is much more to this story.Once again we see the salmon issue being raised only as a smokescreen for social, economic, and political manoeuvrings:

During the early eighties the Quebec Government under the leadership of Prime Minister René Lévesque orchestrated a bold move to stop the Indians of the Restigouche Reserve from blocking the estuary of the Restigouche River with nets.Separatist Prime Minister Lévesque ordered his Minister of Loisir Chasse et Pêche, the Honourable Lucien Lessard, to raid the Restigouche Indian reserve and arrest all the Indians (they termed warriors) who were involved in fishing with nets and also seize all of their fishing equipment.About one hundred policemen and one hundred game wardens were mobilised in Matapedia. They set up their headquarters in the conference room at my place of business. Quebec Provincial Police helicopters were present on the property along with dozens of police cars, dozens of game warden trucks and paddy-wagons.

As a former president of the Society responsible for the operation of the Quebec side of the Restigouche River Basin and also former director of the Quebec Salmon Federation, I advised the Quebec Government Delegation that based on my experiences, I did not think it was a good idea to proceed with the plan of raiding the Restigouche Reserve, I offered other alternatives but without success.

As the Quebec Delegation was finalising its plans for the raid, Ottawa was also planning representations of its own. The Lévesque Government being a separatist party was considered by Ottawa as the enemy. There is absolutely no question about it; Ottawa wanted by any means to take all available opportunities of derailing the separatist party of Quebec.

This said . . .

No one realized it at the time, but Ottawa's plan of derailing the Quebec government raid on the Restigouche Indian Reserve, would set-up the stage for most present policies governing Canada's Aboriginal People today.

The honourable Pierre Eliot Trudeau then Prime Minister of Canada ordered his Minister of Indian Affairs the Honourable John Monroe, to go on to the Restigouche Indian Reserve in advance of the Quebec law enforcement action and to make absolutely sure that a politically embarrassing reception awaited the arrival of the Quebec Delegation.The plan was that Minister Monroe was to get all of the warriors either out of the reserve or to stay hidden in their houses. So when the Quebec Delegation arrived to conduct the raid on the reserve, they would be confronted by all of the women and children of the reserve along with the media rather than by the "warriors".The Federal Government had set-up the Quebec Delegation perfectly since it was ridiculously unacceptable for this paramilitary force to confront the women and children especially in front of the media.Then Minister Monroe told the Quebec Delegation: First Nation People are under federal jurisdiction, you have no business here on this reserve.Thus Prime Minister Trudeau's plan made it impossible for the Quebec Delegation to accomplish their mission thus it was aborted.

Following this "raid" the Honourable John Monroe while puffing on the peace pipe with the Chief and his elders said, "see how Quebec would treat you if it was separated from Canada . . ." You support us and we will support you.

As the Quebec Delegation returned to Quebec City and met with Prime Minister Lévesque, it was then clear they had made an enormous political mistake.Realizing they had now made the First Nation People of Quebec their enemies, they had a situation that needed to be corrected immediately. There is no question that they needed to have the First Nation People on their side if they were to succeed with the separation of Quebec from Canada.

Quebec quickly tried to re-conciliate with the First Nation People by giving very generous programs of all sorts and financial assistance.On many occasions the Quebec Government would grant First Nation People such special privileges that these would even cause considerable resentments among many rural Quebecers who had been living under difficult economic conditions for a long period of time.

Meanwhile the Federal Government was keeping a very close eye on the evolution of the Quebec's separatist party and the developments with the First Nation's People, as they did not want to lose their public relations gains made during the Quebec Delegation's raid on the Restigouche Reserve. Ottawa, seeing that Quebec was making substantial headway and regaining the First Nation People to their cause, felt they needed to also make bold moves to stop the separatist party's progress.

The Federal Government decided if it was good for Quebec to give to the First Nation People, then it should be good for Ottawa also. From then on the race was on for who was going to give the most. First Nation People quickly realised that Ottawa and Quebec had now made them the buffer between the French Separatists of Quebec and English Canada.A position they still cherish very much today.

Canadians can now recognise the essence behind why our federal and provincial governments are so afraid and hesitant of getting involved when a First Nation Conflict is on.

Getting back to one of most serious issues that has been bothering me for a long time, I would like to point out once again, for the benefit of the record, and for the information of my fellow anglers, that there is serious lack of transparency in the manner in which directors of our federations and foundations and other so-called conservation groups are elected.This lack of transparency allows the existence of conflicts of interest to and the promotion of private agendas by those in charge.

At the annual meeting of the Corporation de Gestion des Rivières Matapédia et Patapédia, I was shocked to see their voting policies in electing their directors. At that year's meeting the president of election was chosen hurriedly, then nomination of directors was commenced, followed by the election whereby members would enter the names of the proposed directors of their choice on a voting paper sheet supplied.These papers were picked up and counted only by the secretary, the chief administrator and the selected election president.Then the president of election announced the results.

Following the announcement of the results, some unsatisfied or maybe suspicious members requested whether they could check the ballot count themselves.Permission was **vigorously** refused. Other members then asked about the vote counts for each director.This was also refused.

It was so evident that this election process was orchestrated solely to keep total control of power within a certain predetermined group. I had heard from fellow anglers often before about these kinds of election practices throughout the salmon conservation establishment.Now I recognized them as facts!Later I will address this same issue concerning the Atlantic Salmon Federation's total control of power by not letting anglers participate in the voting process, but for right now I must briefly return to my soapbox to discuss another outrageous story about clear cut logging.

At a meeting in the spring of 1995, the Corporation de Gestation des Rivières Matapédia et Patapédia, (C.G.R.M.P.) were laughing and clapping like little kids who had been given lollipops. Wouldn't you know! They had just received a ten-thousand-dollar donation from a local logging company!

Under the management of Mr. Al Carter (brother to Wilfred Carter, of the Atlantic Salmon Federation) even the prestigious Restigouche Salmon Club joined in the clear-cut logging frenzy.Al was only too pleased to sacrifice thousands of acres of virgin forest owned by the RSC, at times letting his men clear-cut right down near the river. **Unbelievable!**The local population living along the Restigouche River are very well aware of these massive clear-cutting operations conducted on the properties of the Restigouche Salmon Club.How can one expect to promote change when even these riparian owners join in the frenzy over massive clear-cutting operations?Has the money dulled their senses or what?We will continue to examine the actions of the clubs and the federations and discuss the available evidence that indicates very clearly that things are not what they should be.

In a series of articles, which appeared in the Saint John Telegraph Journal, Al Carter boasted of how well he was managing the forest and portion of river owned by the Restigouche Salmon Club. Mr. Phillip Lee, writer for the newspaper, wrote an article published on November 8, 1995, following an interview with Al Carter.

'' **We wouldn't even think of cutting a single tree along the river**, `` said Cater," **and for firewood we go beyond the mountain not to disrupt the environment.** ``

Who in the world does Al Carter thinks he is fooling?Is it possible he believes that people living along the Restigouche River are too dumb to figure out what is going on?

Phillip Lee has to be some kind of journalist!How can he have possibly written a story so important to the future of the Restigouche River, and not do the proper research?How is it possible that he did not know all along that the Restigouche Salmon Club was involved in massive clear-cutting of their land?

Following these articles in the Telegraph Journal, Philip Lee was named editor of the prestigious Atlantic Salmon Journal.Is it possible these articles may have had something to do with his promotion?

The first logging operation initiated by Al Carter, while managing the Restigouche Salmon Club, was to clear-cut a virgin forest, including the side hills, and islands of the brook which supplies the water reservoir for the village of Matapédia.He might as well have dropped a bomb on the village!For over a decade following the deforestation of the reservoir, the village had nothing to drink but muddy water after every rainfall, which caused massive quantities of mud and silt to be carried into the reservoir.The taxpayers later paid thousands of dollars for the required reservoir dredging operation.I expect that Al Carter and the billionaire owners of the RSC got paid well for the trees that came from that virgin forest but I do not expect they lost much sleep over the catastrophe they caused to working people of Matepedia.

To show the additional costs and inconveniences caused to local residents and businesses, just consider the small case of my Hotel Restigouche: After each rainfall we had to flush all coffee, ice and hot water machines used for the restaurant, clean baths, toilets, and sinks, twice each day for our seventy five bath rooms, etc.Drinking water had to be brought in from elsewhere for the kitchen and dining room.The above inconveniences cost the Hotel over $50,000.00 in damage, all of it done without a cent of compensation from the RSC.

One can go on and on about the incestuous relations between the Restigouche Salmon Club (and other private Clubs) and The Atlantic Salmon Federation and the giant forestry operators of Eastern Canada!I hate to engage in name calling but here's what other think and say:

Richard Firth, the man in charge of managing the Matapédia and the portion of the Restigouche River on the Quebec side, at a meeting during a discussion on clear-cut-logging was asked . . . ´´ Why doesn't your organization try to stop these abusive logging practices that are destroying our salmon rivers? `` His answer was, - ´´ If I were to interfere in any way to try to control logging in this area I would end up dead, and I do not mean dead as an expression.I mean six feet underground! ``

I have been accumulating and developing the information in this book for years.Many times I have sent out letters and studies and papers to all the various media.I have even tried television talk shows.I have never succeeded in obtaining any media coverage with the exception of the Maine Sportsman, (New England's Largest Outdoor Publication), with Harry Vanderwiede, the editor.

Harry is a good friend of mine and published a substantial part of my logging story in his magazine during March of 1995.The following spring when Harry arrived at my place of business for his spring fishing expedition, he entered my office wearing a cap with the International Paper Co. logo on it and a big smirk on his face.He realized immediately that I had noticed the cap and said . . .´´ Hey Pete! These people are now subsidizing my television program big time!What am I supposed to do? . .Refuse them? `` No, Harry, I answered.´´ If I were in your financial situation I would probably do the same thing".

In a hand-written letter addressed to me from Doctor David Suzuki, he states:

"We have done stories on clear-cut-logging before and have been hammered by the forest industry, right now the CBC is under siege and is terrified of getting into more controversy".

Pierre D`Amours of Matapédia is an experienced salmon biologist, with a Masters Degree in Salmon Biology.He has spent his lifetime since he was just a young boy with his father on the Matapédia and the Restigouche where both guided salmon anglers for years.

Pierre had one really bad habit when making a report on salmon conservation . . . He tells it like it is!It seems that the truth is not always well accepted by the salmon conservation establishment. Salmon biologists who tell the whole truth just do not seem to have jobs . . .

The Restigouche Salmon Club sponsored scholarship for Pierre`s education as they do for many young local students who show potential in the science of biology.Is all this done to promote future conservation of the environment, or is it done to have these future biologists eating out of their hands?

For over a century the clubs of the Restigouche River have been promoting their clubs as the economic backbone of the Restigouche Watershed. What residents have failed to understand is that it is not the clubs that are the economic backbone of the Restigouche Watershed, but rather the river and its salmon that is the resource, not the clubs.As a matter of fact the clubs of the Restigouche River have had a negative impact on the local economy.

Good businessmen have always known that to be successful in business one must be at the right location, Matapedia is perfectly located, entrance to the maritime, the USA, the Gaspe Peninsula and major centres of the province of Quebec. Why is it that Matapedia today only has a population of less than seven hundred residents when it should be a small city? It is natural for the clubs of the Restigouche River not to want development and keep the riverside in a wild state, in other words the fewer people and development around the best it is for these clubs.Here's just one example of what I'm trying to demonstrate:As Quebec biggest food distributor "Provigo" was trying to implement a distribution centre in Matapedia, creating over two hundred jobs. Imagine an establishment coming to your town creating jobs for half the population of the whole town, this would be unbelievably good news.While here in Matapedia the Restigouche Salmon Club did all it could to stop this project from going ahead. It took two municipal counsellors to meet with Mr. Al Carter then manager of the Restigouche Salmon Club.Mr. Andre Beaulieu and Mr. Bernard Mills had to make it very clear to Mr. Carter that if the Restigouche Salmon Club kept on blocking this project the population would be turned against them creating enormous problems for their Club.

Tourists travelling the Matapedia Valley and using a GPS system for directions will find to their surprise that the Restigouche River Basin (the portion normally shown in blue for water on the GPS screen does not show for this major river system when elsewhere minor river system appear on the GPS screen) is excluded from most if not all GPS systems, and when searching in the Matapedia vicinity for a restaurant, a service station or a room to stay, Matapedia again is totally excluded. Surprisingly a very small service station with a single regular gas only pump located some twenty miles in the backcountry behind Matapedia is listed. The most popular dining facility (The Salmon Lodge) located just across the river from Matapedia on the New Brunswick side of the river bank is also not listed, while every dinning and small takeouts in the Campbellton to Tide Head area are entirely listed.

A recent addition to the original building of 40 rooms with bath, 4 spacious social halls makes the Restigouche one of the leading hotels of the Province of Quebec and the largest and most exclusive of the Gaspé tour.

We give special attention to our dining room service.

Fresh sea-foods and fresh farm and dairy products rich in vitamins are served daily.

The "Restigouche Hotel" Matapedia, Que.

THE RESTIGOUCHE HOTEL

An up-to-date fire-proof building with all modern accommodation, the RESTIGOUCHE HOTEL has its doors open to the travelling public the year round. Located at the very meeting point of the Matapedia and Ristigouche rivers, our guests can enjoy right from their rooms or from the veranda very fine scenery.

In a quiet and secluded spot the RESTIGOUCHE HOTEL at Matapedia, with all the comforts of the city (hot and cold running water in every room, rooms with bath, electric light and bell service, beer and wine served with meals) is the ideal place for anyone seeking rest and tranquility while on vacation. Here everyone will find service and courtesy together with all the comforts of home.

The Restigouche Hotel in 1937 Brochure today it is considered a Historical Monument offering one of the highest quality accommodations on the Gaspé tour

The Restigouche Garage in Matapedia is a full service centre, for transport trucks, RV's and car repairs, professional mechanics, welders, a huge tire inventory, a well stocked auto parts, towing, diesel and gasoline, you name it, they have it, why then are these important businesses from the village of Matapedia not listed on GPS navigation systems?

There cannot possibly be any question that some private or governmental interests have manipulated these GPS map systems to exclude Matapedia from most, if not all, GPS map systems.It is as if someone does not want to make it easy for visitors to find our village.I wonder now who these people are, and what they expect to gain by depriving the village of Matapedia of visitors.After thinking about this myself, and talking with others, we can only believe that the powerful interests who control the Restigouche Salmon Club(s) are strong enough to accomplish their objective of isolating the Restigouche and the Matapedia rivers from the outside world.Those of us who live here are not so happy to have the visitors, who are our livelihoods, be discouraged from finding us.As if this is not bad enough the story gets worse, much worse.

It is a well established fact that since 1974 the village of Matapedia has been subjected to very severe flooding and ice-jams on a regular basis during the spring thaw.We can prove without the slightest doubt that these relatively recent annual ice flooding events are entirely due to manmade causes.It will not be difficult to understand, and will not require any new science to see very clearly the causes and effects.

When the McDonald government in 1881 gave Lord Mount Stephen and his company, the Canadian Pacific Railway, the contract to build the railroad across Canada, it was obvious that to complete such a gigantic project in only six years, there could be no time wasted on assessing environmental impacts.That is why government authorized the railway project to build a 4300 foot dike with its highest elevation point reaching close to forty feet in height smack in middle of the Restigouche River bed. This dike also includes a bridge with four huge pillars awkwardly slanted to the water currents causing a severe constriction and slowdown of the river flow.And if that was not enough, the Quebec and the New Brunswick governments authorized the construction of a new inter-provincial bridge, erected in 1973 five hundred metres below the present (CNR) railway bridge joining the two provinces.This bridge added four more giant pillars; further obstructing the river, and in addition to this they added a second causeway for the Gaspé railway entering the river bed above and below the bridge, causing massive restriction of water and ice movements in the Matapedia sector.Immediately following the construction (summer of 1973) of the new inter-provincial bridge, every spring, from 1974 on, it has been a yearly event to have major ice flooding in the village of Matapedia which is located just above these manmade obstructions in the Restigouche River bed.

Let there be no doubt that one of the main objectives of this book is to report the failures of irresponsible government planning wherever such failures can be proved.None of our successive governments will report on their own failures.That is unheard of.We hear about only successes and we get "spin" and damage control on the failures.When was the last time any of us have ever heard the government accepting responsibility for creating even a small fiasco, let alone a catastrophe such as the horrendous mess they have created on the Restigouche and for the village of Matapedia. This refusal to acknowledge responsibility for these mistakes, effectively denies any chance of fair economic assistance and appropriate financial aid to owners of large buildings similar to my place of business leaving us struggling to stay afloat.This simply adds gross economic injustice to our list of grievances emanating from our government's total disregard for meaningful environmental protection.The pursuit of a reasonable degree of justice is the essence of this publication.

4300 foot causeway (dike) smack in the Restigouche Riverbed

Matapedia has coped relatively well during the first half a century after the completion of the railway dike with ice flooding. Residents have rebuilt on higher elevations and prevented their buildings from water and ice damage.But as totally out of control clear-cut-logging appeared in the early 1960's, a third manmade and unpredictable event for the residents of Matapedia surfaced, with a dramatic increase in the amount of run-off water yield during the spring thaw following these massive deforestation events which are very well documented in aerial photos. The residents of Matapedia now were forced to suffer though devastating and unprecedented annual 450% increases in spring water flows in the Restigouche River Basin (based on actual water flow measurements).Obviously governments are entirely responsible for these manmade events.By not enforcing forestry laws and regulations, they have failed us all and allowed massive destruction to the environment and private property to occur.

They have the moral and legal obligation to take all possible measures to prevent or repair the harm they have caused to the residents of this village.Because of their outrageous negligence in this matter, our governments have the unconditional and total obligation to fully compensate all affected parties for the damages caused by each of these events.

This said, I am very grateful to the Honourable Marcel Landry of the PQ government for saving Matapedia from the total destruction of the village by ice flooding.Mr Landry as MLA for our county made all the necessary arrangements (as of spring of 1995) to employ a one hundred ton hovercraft to break the ice in the lower Restigouche every spring. This action of breaking ice in the lower Restigouche was an overwhelming success and totally eliminating ice flooding from occurring in the village of Matapedia.

For unexplained and or undisclosed reasons from our government leaders during the spring of 2008 following a record winter snow accumulation, with all evidences indicating of a possible catastrophic ice flood for the village of Matapedia, **the hovercraft did not show up**.This is unquestionably an act of criminal negligence from our governments.Severe sanctions need to be implemented against these irresponsible government leaders as they have totally neglected their responsibilities to protecting the public, **a public they have placed in this position in the first place**.There are many who believe that this was an attempt to destroy the village of Matapedia and to render the village unfit for residents and business.Wiping out the village would give rise to government payouts for losses to the residents and business, and a massive exodus of the population, leaving the land and whatever structures are left over to be turned over to the private interests and their government cronies, thus completing the privatization of the entire Restigouche and Matapedia river systems.Yes, we are of course, speaking here of a horrendous criminal conspiracy.

In recent years, three of the best veteran guides of the Restigouche Salmon Club were in my office and one said: "The RSC always wants to make sure that the guides on June the 1st are god-damn good and hungry".In my opinion, Guy Moores was (in my lifetime) the best and most accomplished fishing guide working for the Restigouche River, he was a sort of intellectual, very well informed person, a man who could quickly analyse what was happening in his surroundings, in other words he was no fool!On many occasions Guy would refer to the RSC members . . ."They're nothing but a bunch of tramps".William "Billy" Falls the owner of Falls Outboard Marine in Matapedia, veteran guide and manager of two salmon fishing clubs on the Restigouche River, when referring to the new members of the RSC he'd call them . . ."Ontario Bums". He says that since the Canadian's have moved into the RSC it's run on the cheap, "you'd swear they were all on welfare".

Enough name calling for now.As you can see everyone has strong feelings about this subject.Let's return to the discussion to a higher level and address the socio economic implications to the general public, by having such a small group of people controlling so much of the government and the economy.

Riparian Rights

It is not clear how or why the Canadian Government during the late 1870's, to early 1880's have released the Riparian Rights on many of our Canadian Rivers. Most of the riparian rights throughout Canada were acquired by extremely wealthy Americans, whom many are still owners today.For those of you who are not familiar with riparian rights, riparian rights are the ownership of the portion of land that the river flows on.In other words the owner of a riparian right on a Salmon River owns the bottom of the river, and usually one or two rods length of land from the high water mark on that portion of river.If you hanker your canoe or walk the beach on a riparian owned portion of river, you are technically then trespassing.

During a conversation a few decades back with uncle John Paul Dubé, (co-ordinator of sport salmon fishing for the province of Quebec) he mentioned that during the mid to late1700s, a law was passed by the Canadian Government stating to the effect: "All navigable Canadian Waterways are the property of the Government of Canada and cannot be owned by an individual".As far as John Paul knew then, that law is still applicable today.The meaning of Navigable Waters meant, any waterway which can float a canoe (boat) including occupants and cargo for travelling from one place to another. That was considered Navigable Waters. Here in Eastern Canada Riparian Rights are considered as private property by their owners, and when a sale takes place it is sold as such. Since it is private property, why is it that Riparian Rights are not part of most municipal taxation roles?And for the few that are evaluated the amount are ridiculously low, thus municipalities bordering salmon rivers have lost millions in taxation revenues since the release of Riparian Rights in the 1880's.

It should also be mentioned here that the Riparian Rights owned by clubs of the Restigouche River have never been properly evaluated for municipal tax purposes. By not properly evaluating these Riparian Rights, the clubs of the Restigouche River have evaded paying over a $100,000,000.00 in municipal property tax since the early 1880's. It is hard to believe that the mayors of these villages bordering the Restigouche River did not know that the Riparian Rights could be legally evaluated for municipal tax purposes

In a discussion with Uncle George Greene after he retired as manager of the Restigouche Salmon Club, I asked, how much is the million-dollar pool evaluated for municipal taxes?His answer, I don't think that it is evaluated at all!Imagine that! Just the million dollar pool by itself, (only one kilometre of Restigouche River) a property that the Restigouche Salmon Club refused $1,000,000.00 for in the early 1900s. What should a treasure like this be evaluated for today?The same hold true for the entire Restigouche River Basin.The multi-billionaire club owners have succeeded in evading something in the neighbourhood of a million dollars of taxes (based on today's fair value) on their riparian water rights every year since 1880. This is quite a public relations accomplishment to say the least; one of the most economically depressed areas in North America, subsidizing summer parties for the wealthiest people on the planet.Only an uninformed public or, in the case of the people of New Brunswick, a misinformed public, would allow a situation as unfair as this to continue unchallenged.

Today the Coporation de Gestion des Rivières Matapedia et Patapedia (C.G.R.M.P.) located in Causapscal thirty-five miles upstream from Matapedia, have or could have cunningly made (since it is kept highly confidential)the following arrangements with the clubs of the Restigouche River mainly the Restigouche Salmon Club.

First, Causapscal is located in the Matapedia County and Matapedia is located in the Bonaventure County. Secondly, people from both of these two towns do not know each other, they are strangers. Thirdly, ever since salmon fishing was practised on the Restigouche River Basin, the town of Causapscal never received one cent from the fishing clubs of the Bonaventure County.

The C.G.R.M.P. who now detains control of the Restigouche River Quebec side, have or could have managed by hooks or by crooks with the Restigouche Salmon Club to have the Riparian Water Rights of the Clubs of the Restigouche River turned into Fauna Zones.By turning the Club's Water Rights into Fauna Zones the C.G.R.M.P. just with a simple signature on a contract to that effect with the clubs of the Restigouche River could receive an annual payment of some $250,000,00 for the next twenty-five to fifty years.And the local population from the Bonaventure County would get most likely nothing.What troubles me with the above deal, is how in the world did the mayors of these five small villages of the Bonaventure County could accept that their constituency would lose $50,000.00 annually each in municipal tax revenues? To me this is incomprehensible and does not pass the "sniff test".

If just 17 miles of the Pulaski "Salmon River" in up-state New York can generate some $25,000,000 of economic annual windfall for the area with a run of 250,000 fish. The Restigouche River Basin has some four hundred miles of river where salmon can be fished and it generates less than $5,000,000.00 annually. Imagine what all the rivers on the East Coast of Canada could generate if salmon runs were what they should be in the millions of fish?

The Clubs on the Restigouche River were the founding backbone of the ASA (Atlantic Salmon Association) over fifty years ago, and still today (under the name of Atlantic Salmon Federation) considered its main pillar.Unfortunately, some of these very same groups have abused the salmon daily limits for decades prior to when the Catch & Release program was introduced on the Restigouche and on all of eastern Canada's Rivers.I am reminded of the old saying:"No one has more virtue than a reformed whore."

For decades the portion of Restigouche River exclusively owned by Clubs, mostly Restigouche Salmon Club, it was routine to take double the daily limits under the pretence one license for each side of the river was required. (The portion of the Restigouche River that separates New Brunswick and Quebec)

The clubs took advantage of that loophole in the law and doubled the daily salmon limit, killing four salmon per day per member.

Two salmon were taken on the Quebec side of the river and two on the New Brunswick side.Also, at one club, where guests routinely took their limits early in the day (during the early to mid seventies which I will talk extensively about later) the guides were ordered out again on the river to catch their limits on their own licenses.Upon their return to the club they had to leave their fish at the canning factory located in back of the camp, where someone was appointed the task of canning and affixing personalized custom design labelling on the cans, which were than taken back to the States by the owners or their guests.

Many of these members thus had four salmon a day limit, while everyone else on the Atlantic Coast was allowed only two.

During the period following the lifting of the commercial nets in the Bay des Chaleurs from 1972 to 1978, so many fish were killed by many of these club members, that at times icehouses were so full of salmon that many would spoil and had to be buried.Could not these fish have been given to the needy of the area?

With the constant slumping sales of salmon **season** licenses, (in Quebec from over 25,000 **season** licenses in the mid seventies to 7,000 **resident season** licenses at present.)It is evident that it is becoming more and more noticeable that our Governments on the East Coast have lost their incentive to save the Atlantic salmon.Non resident anglers are not returning to our rivers due to the poor angling.The New Brunswick resident anglers are pouting about the introduction of Catch & Release and have abandoned their salmon fishing.The resident angler's involvement to save salmon is rapidly declining, thus replaced by others who seem to have different interest or priorities.It is evident . . . havoc on our salmon is only decades away!

When Catch & Release was introduced in 1984, the Restigouche River was in much better shape fish wise than the Matapédia.Today the Matapédia with the killing limit of one mature salmon per day is in just as good shape fish wise as the Restigouche, and we must consider, too, that the Matapédia has much more fishing pressure than the Restigouche.Larger fish have also increased in numbers (as of 1995 not today when this portion of the book was written) on the Matapédia, in comparison to the early eighties when most salmon had dropped to less than fifteen pounds.

The Province of Quebec's present method permits keeping one mature fish as the daily limits and allows one to continue fishing if the first catch is a grilse, for a total of two fish per day for the months of June and July.And if at the end of July, the river doesn´t meet the required number of fish to ensure a sustainable reproduction quota following a fish count, then Catch & Release is introduced for the balance of the season.

Veteran guide Lawrence Gray releasing a nice Restigouche salmon

In my opinion, it is nonsense! More fish will be killed during the hot water conditions of August with the introduction of Catch Release, than would be if a limit of one fish a day were continued on rivers that show hot water problems like the Miramichi and the Restigouche.

To close or introduce Catch & Release on rivers that show less salmon than the required quota for sustainable reproduction, or due to hot water problem during mid to late season, is, in my opinion, a foolish decision.A mistake like that shows lack of imagination, incompetence, and poor business administration sense from our conservation leaders.Closing salmon rivers to angling will only leave them wide-open to poaching, as there will be no presence of anglers for protection and also devastating to the local economy.

Could it be that a certain group of salmon anglers have a lot to gain by a reduction of anglers on our rivers?I will explain in a following chapter.

Rivers with very large salmon and hot water problem like the Restigouche do not benefit at all from Catch & Release during July and August.Rivers with smaller fish and much colder water can **maybe** deliver some results if the angler catches his limit and limits his catch.

David Anderson, while Minister of Canadian Fisheries, has stated clearly during a televised debate, that "Catch & Release is not the answer to have more salmon return to the Skeena and the Thompson Rivers in B.C."Mortality, and some yet not completely understood interference with the reproduction cycle and possible contamination through open wounds, have to be considered.

Catch & Release, is in my opinion, here to stay for certain anglers whom prefer not to consume salmon.More and more anglers have learned to appreciate the extra time it can give them to practice their favourite sport and that is fine, but, one must not assume it is the answer to save our salmon, like the Atlantic Salmon Federation is promoting.ASF has its very own reason for promoting Catch & Release, you'll understand later.

Paul Leonard playing and releasing a salmon during the spring season in icy water

Guide extraordinaire Peter Firth with a GIANT spring Restigouche Salmon

In early July during the second year of Catch & Release, Uncle John Paul Dubé (coordinator of salmon fishing for the province of Quebec) and I decided to travel the Restigouche River by motor canoe from Matapedia to the Million Dollar Pool 39 miles up-river from Matapedia.I had mentioned to J. P. during the winter of the high mortality rate from salmon released during the previous summer, so he wanted to investigate for himself.During our travel to the Million Dollar Pool we observed forty-two dead salmon of which only two showed signs of furunculosis; all the other fish had died apparently from exaution and less likely from other unexplained causes. As we arrived at Big Crosspoint the warden Jimmy Haley was in, so we droped in to pay him a visit.During our conversation with Jimmy he mentioned that he had received order to retrive all dead salmon from the river, he had a sixteen foot pole equiped with a hook at the end to help him make deep-water retrieving. All dead fish collected had to be burried in the woods along the river, as we got closer to Million Dollar Pool both of us could not believe the smell of dead fish in the air. Considering that J. P. and I might only have sighted half of the actual dead fish, since we were traveling at fairly high speed with a twenty-five HP motor.Considering also that the wardens were retrieving the dead fish, it is conceivable that the dead fish count could have been considerably higher.

I am including for you the following information so that you will be properly informed and in a better position to take a stand on future regulations concerning Catch & Release.

Following the announcement of the new salmon daily limit of one fish a day for all rivers in Quebec, (Salmon or a grilse would be the daily limit for the 1984 season, at the FQSA 1983 fall meeting in Matane.) it was also announced that the portion of the Restigouche River separating Quebec and New Brunswick all owned by **clubs,** would no longer be permitted to double the daily limits as they have been abusing it for decades.

This meant that the clubs (don't forget they are the guys who seem to control the ASF) would no longer benefit from the loophole in the law, which tolerated them to double the daily limit. From now on, clubs from Tide Head to the mouth of the Patapédia River would be compelled to follow the same regulations as everyone else on the Atlantic Coast.

The fact that private fishing clubs control so much of the salmon fishing water in New Brunswick and Quebec is working to the detriment of obtaining funding for major public works projects to improve and restore our rivers because the private owners control the political agenda and they don't want anything to change.

British Columbia, Washington and Oregon states where rivers don't freeze-up have no problem with **secondary** erosion, (massive ice jamming that can produce up to ten folds the damage to our salmon habitat than primary erosion) and still these rivers are in peril.The difference on the West Coast, is that the anglers, commercial fishermen and environment groups are better informed today, and participate much more than we do here on the East Coast to promote and defend the environment.We need to **accurately** inform our commercial fishermen and anglers here in Eastern Canada, as they have been kept in the dark by the ASF, and the FQSA for too long.

The West Coast has just been granted (as of 1996) by the Federal Government $100,000.000.00 to repair the damage of erosion on the Thompson and the Skeena Rivers.**What about our rivers here in Eastern Canada that are falling apart from totally out of control logging?**

I have to raise my hat to the people of the Margaree Valley in Nova Scotia for their outstanding work controlling the structure of their rivers.These people have a way of looking after their rivers that is decades ahead of any river organizations here in Quebec or New Brunswick.I am sure the secret to their success is the fact that the local population is in charge of the river so everyone is working to protect its interest for future generations.It seems the more a river is owned by non-resident "**Clubs**" the less it is looked after.

Robert Chiasson on the Margaree

The Margaree has the most fishing pressure of any river I know, and still manages to have near sufficient fish left to spawn and meet sustainable reproduction requirement.Results could be much more impressive if they banned the use of sinking lines during the summer when water levels are low, and increased the daily access fee, which is ridiculously cheap.It is the only river I know of as of today in which all pools give the fly line a uniform natural flow travelling across its undisturbed water currents, offering the angler perfect presentation every-time due to appropriate habitat restoration. . .

What a pleasure it is to fish the Margaree! . . Especially when one has the privilege to fish it during quieter periods.The Margaree is a very prosperous river due to public access to the entire river. It serves as an important economic leverage for the local tourist establishment, which is the essence of its success.What are we waiting for to follow the Margaree example, and restructure our river habitats and open up all fishing to public access?

I can remember during the mid to late seventies, when we did not have to spend one cent on advertising to fill up our rivers with happy anglers during the summer.Today, we have to spend a fortune on advertising, trying to entice anglers to return to our rivers in Quebec.Even with huge promotion efforts, the results are not encouraging at all.Thanks to the introduction of a spring and fall salmon season that has partly compensated for some of the lost revenues.

Atlantic Salmon Federation members received a **NEWS** letter for members.(You will find a copy on the following pages **please read them before continuing.**)

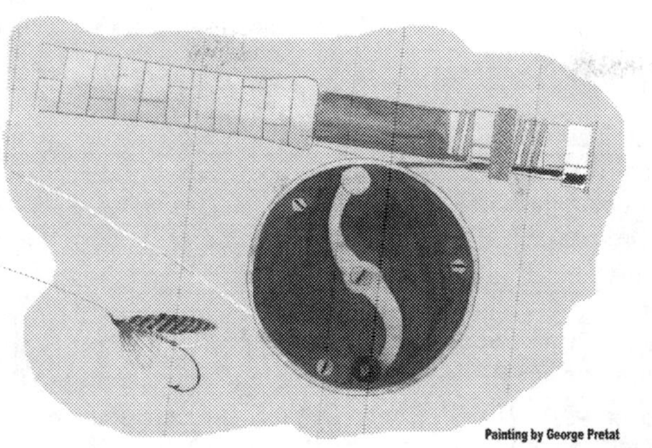

Painting by George Pretat

News

FOR MEMBERS

IRVING/ASF RESEARCH PROVIDING NEW INFORMATION ON RESTIGOUCHE WATERSHED

St. Andrews. In May, J. D. Irving, Limited and the Atlantic Salmon Federation began the third year of a joint research program to conserve and restore Atlantic salmon populations in the Little Main Restigouche River and Clearwater Brook, a tributary of the Main Southwest Miramichi River. Researchers are gathering reliable data on the counts of Atlantic salmon fry, parr and returning adults for all areas of the test rivers. One problem researchers face on the Restigouche River, one of the top salmon rivers in the world, is that there are no reliable stock assessment statistics. The Irving\ASF research, a cooperative effort involving industry, the University of New Brunswick, various conservation organizations, the federal Department of Fisheries and Oceans (DFO) and New Brunswick's Department of Natural Resources and Energy (DNRE), is changing that.

In 1997, researchers installed a counting fence on the Little Main Restigouche River. Dr. Frederick Whoriskey, ASF's Vice President of Research and Environment, states, "Good information is the key to successful salmon management. Now, for the first time ever, we are able to count and record data on every fish that enters or exits this tributary of the Restigouche which is about 19% of the total Restigouche watershed." Dr. Whoriskey believes that a salmon count here is an excellent indicator of returns to the whole river system.

During 1998, information is being gathered about salmon movements and juvenile densities. From this data, researchers will determine what areas need enhancement and then attempt to optimize salmon production through management plans that address the specific needs of rivers in locations that require help. Biologists will use information gathered on these rivers to manage salmon populations in other river systems as well. According to Dr. Whoriskey, the salmon runs are much larger this year. In 1997, researchers counted 69 grilse and 22 multi-sea-winter (MSW) salmon at the counting fence on Boston Brook. This year, they counted more than four times as many grilse (384) and almost eight times more MSW salmon (173). (see graph attached)

This information is being distributed to the Department of Fisheries and Oceans and the Department of Natural Resources and Energy. DFO has never carried out in-season assessments for the Restigouche River because it lacked reliable data on returning Restigouche salmon stocks. This year DFO programs could determine in-season returns on the Miramichi and relaxed catch and release restrictions in mid July, the same could not be done on the Restigouche. ASF's research project is now providing DFO with the information it needs for in-season assessments and responsible river management. DFO can implement stricter management measures, if need be, before salmon numbers drop to crisis levels or relax restrictions during increased runs. The information will also allow scientists to more accurately estimate egg depositions and predict returns for ensuing years.

ATLANTIC SALMON FEDERATION
P.O. Box 429, St. Andrews, New Brunswick, Canada E0G 2X0 × P.O. Box 807, Calais, Maine, USA 04619-0807
Tel. (506) 529-1025 Fax (506) 529-4438 E-mail asf@nbnet.nb.ca

J. D Irving, Limited has shown great foresight in sustaining natural resources through well-executed reforestation programs, realizing that maintaining the health of the forests ensures a continuing supply to meet future product demands. The company's philosophy of sustainable development goes beyond trees and encompasses all aspects of the environment, including the rivers and the fish populations they support

"We are eager to learn what new approaches we should take to better protect and enhance salmon habitat in the rivers and streams that run throughout our woodland operations." states Jim Irving "We believe Dr. Whoriskey's research on the Little Main Restigouche will serve as an important benchmark for enhancing salmon habitat around the world."

Dr Whoriskey concludes, "Responsible development, involving industry, governments and conservation partners, bodes well for the future. If an industry leader like J. D. Irving is willing to invest its resources to improve the environment, then we can hope that other companies will see the environmental and economic benefits of managing resources wisely and follow the Irving example."

BOSTON BROOK COUNTING FENCE

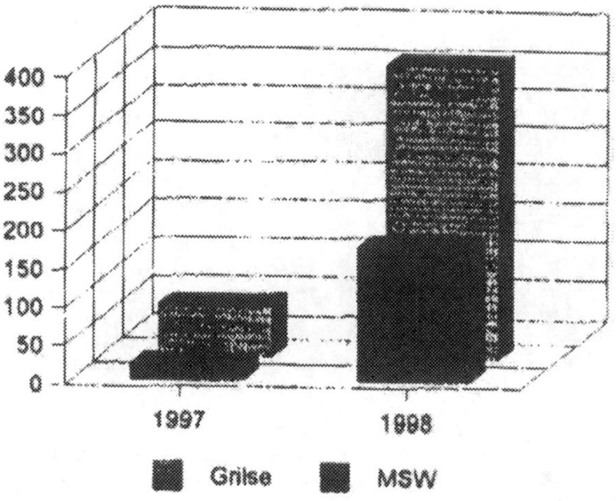

	1997	1998
Grilse	69	386
MSW	22	173

Doesn't this make you wonder where all the millions in donations given to the ASF have gone?Can you believe this!The ASF classifies the Restigouche River as one of the top Atlantic salmon rivers in the world, and still after 50 years of supposedly having taken care of our salmon resources they are still without a record of fish entering the Restigouche.To top it all, the ASF is working hand in hand with the most aggressive logging operator in the province of New Brunswick, a company very well known for its devastating environmental record. And now, the ASF is campaigning to raise the Irving Company to the top of the pedestal as a model to follow for conservation.

It is well known that these companies have been involved for years in massive clear-cutting operations on the Restigouche, the Miramichi River Basins and most rivers on the East Coast causing severe erosion problems, and apparently the ASF and the FQSA have no problems with this.In fact now, all of a sudden, **they are the good guys.**The ASF is portraying the Irving's, the Fraser's, the Roland's as model companies for everyone to follow!This is why those who understand the hypocrisy of what is going on here are bursting at the seams.But you can be sure that I will continue to tell it like it is.

Back to that **Newsletter.**It has to be the worst rubbish and insult to salmon anglers I have ever read on salmon conservation in my entire life!The ASF working hand in hand with the least environmentally friendly logging company in Canada, counting salmon in very small tributaries of the Restigouche River, and actually trying to make its members believe that this is going to save our salmon.

Here is the REALITY of What the Restigouche River Basin really is Today:

One has just to examine the June salmon catch records for the Restigouche River Basin during the mid-seventies, to clearly understand the magnitude of deterioration our June salmon runs have suffered.Our June salmon runs on the Restigouche River Basin, are now some ten or so percent of what they were just twenty-five years ago.June was the month of choice '' **Prime Time"** for anglers, as tens of thousands of fish entered the Restigouche River Basin, all GIANT Atlantic salmon weighing well over twenty pounds.On Glenn Emma, (sector of the Matapédia River) at the end of June in 1974, the average weight of salmon landed was 27 pounds excluding grills.Today we observe anglers fishing for weeks during June before landing their first salmon, compared to the mid-seventies when most anglers returned to camp before noon with a limit of two giant salmon.

The unsurpassed quality of angling on the Restigouche River Basin before the eighties elevated it to the **top** of the **Pedestal** of World Class Angling.**Can we still boast the Restigouche River Basin as the best today?**

A Little Personal History

In the late fifties and the sixties, my father operated the Patapédia River, with five outfitting camps along its banks.Before closing these camps at the end of August, often client anglers were few and he would organize for us each year a week of fishing on the Patapédia.We would, at the same-time, help the guides close camps.My older brother Jacques, cousins Gerald Greene and Maurice Mill, were often part of the group. Our head guide Andrew Haley, accompanied by one of the following guides Bobby Falle, Herby or Ally McNaughton were responsible for us young sports.Once at the camps our job was to split wood and fill the woodsheds full of firewood.After duties were done we had time to fish trout, play horseshoes and other games.

Knowing in advance how good the fishing would be, we would, months before these expeditions make sure the cook, Odilon, at the Hotel saved us two wooden fifty pound butter boxes, one for each canoe to keep our trout in on our August trip to the Patapédia.

The last day of the expedition our voyage consisted of paddling twenty-one miles down the Patapédia River to its mouth, and thirty-nine more miles down the Restigouche to Matapédia where the Hotel is located.

As the guides paddled the long twenty-six foot canoes through the crystal clear wasters of the Patapédia, the young sports admired the countless salmon swimming away shy of the canoe passing through the pools.Thirty to forty deer sightings along the riverbank, a few moose and black bear was a common part of an average day of scenic float down the river.

Once in a while the guides would pole the boat ashore, especially near log jams where trout stacked up like sardines.Trout were so plentiful, that only three or four stops were needed to fill the two wooden butter boxes of fish, averaging from 1/4 pound to 5 pounds.This was of course long before the advent of catch and release fishing.

Royal Bérubé (A friend and fishing companion since childhood)

The guides of the Patapédia considered trout to be pests during these days!Trout could at times make it impossible to catch salmon, as they were too plentiful. The two guided sports often could not fill their salmon limit, as trout constantly grabbed the fly before salmon had a chance to get to it.The constant thrashing around in small pools of the Patapédia, by countless hooked trout, often spoiled the salmon catching chances.

All of us noticed as we drifted the rivers that most evergreen trees had a dull colour to them.We also noticed around camps and as we fished along the shores, many small worms dangling like spiders on a web line from spruce and fir.We did not know at the time what they were, but early the following summer we were informed, that the **DDT**, spraying program was launched to control the spruce bud-worm infestation.

The Author Fishing the Patapédia

Most of the Restigouche River basin received generous showers of DDT, with triumphant results for the logging industry, stopping the spruce budworms epidemic dead in its tracks.

Our next routine expedition on the Patapédia following the DDT spraying turned out to be an extremely disappointing one . . . there was not a trout to be caught; they had all but disappeared! The trout of the Patapédia never returned for years after the DDT spraying programs.Only lately is the population slowly coming back, but a long shot from what it was!

From 1963 on, the deer herd had virtually disappeared from our forest and many point to the DDT as the culprit.

DDT is a carcinogen, (causing cancer) and most if not all guides and wardens working on the Restigouche River Basin during the DDT spraying have died of cancer while their parents, brothers or sisters not exposed to the DDT showed no signs of cancer. Andrew Haley, Jimmy Haley, Bobby Falle, Herby McNaughton, Ally McNaughton and Vernon McNaughton, just to name a few of these exceptionally talented river-men working up-river during the DDT spraying programs on the Restigouche River Basin, had their lives prematurely taken from them as cancer victims, evidently caused by these horrendous environmental crimes.

Predators

NASF (North Atlantic Salmon Funds) from Iceland believes that seals are at the root of the decline of our salmon stocks.In my opinion, they're hitting the nail dead on the head!

Michel Fournier, the man in charge of operating a portion of Anticosti Island, stated clearly during a meeting, that seals were an extremely efficient salmon predator, and had a tremendous impact on the quality of fishing for his rivers.

During a private conversation with Michel, he said,"We hire Treflé, an aboriginal to shoot seals at the mouth of the river, we don't buy bullets for him by the box, we buy them by the case.If we did not shoot the seals at the mouth of the river there would be no salmon entering".

In an article on the Internet"Killer Whales Munch Seals, Save Salmon" stated the following:"The Killer whales, or orcas, were likely drawn by the ample supply of some 1,500 Hood Canal seals, as large as 250 pounds (114kg) on a steady diet of **200 salmon a day**".

Anglers fishing in saltwater either for salmon or other species know very well how seals can attack their catch before getting it to the boat, this fact surprisingly is only unknown to the Atlantic Salmon Federation, I wonder why?

There are at present, according to the North Atlantic Salmon Funds, ten seals for every salmon in the North Atlantic . . . That equals to seal population of around twenty million seals in the North Atlantic.

While we are on the subject of predation, I imagine that the cormorant and the mergansers are just negligible influence on salmon resources, too!

Gilbert Van Rykervorsel, professional under water photographer has a very much different opinion than the one we read about in our federations` magazines.Gilbert has observed mergansers dozens of time working over pools for parrs.His comments were . . . '' **these guys are so efficient at killing parrs that they can make Pack-Man look like a dummy.These guys can totally clean up a pool of parrs in just half a day ``**

Merganser Duck

Mergansers on a Feeding Frenzy

On the Restigouche River a few years back I was observing a flock of over 100 mergansers in one bunch, working McCallum`s pool below the interprovincial Bridge in Matapédia.

All of this is happening without the slightest concern on the part of our salmon Federations.

Biologists proclaim that cormorants and mergansers do not feast on parrs only.They also consume trout . . . and that is part of the natural cycle . . . All of this is true!But what they fail to mention or don't know, is that in the sixties, and for many consecutive years, massive DDT spraying programs took place on the Restigouche River Basin to kill the spruce bud-worms.The DDT spraying programs virtually eliminated the trout population on the Restigouche River Basin.

DDT was also followed by years of spraying of various chemicals (unidentified) on large portions of the Restigouche River Basin.

Today the Aboriginal People at the mouth of the Restigouche are netting most of the returning sea run trout resulting in only a minuscule fraction of the potential trout population being left in the Restigouche River Basin in relation to its natural capacity.So when cormorants and mergansers are by the hundreds on a feeding frenzy . . . it is evident what they are after on the Restigouche!

You know, this reminds me of remarks I so often heard over the years, made by the salmon establishment and biologists telling us that salmon do not feed while in the river . . . Well . . . I agree and understand that salmon do not go around in the river like trout do looking for food. But, for years I have observed salmon feeding for hours on insects in smaller tributaries of the Restigouche. Does this not explain why local poachers have always used for fishing salmon a 5/0 hook stuffed with a bunch of big night crawlers?And they hook lots of salmon, dragging their catch up to the beach with the hook stuck right down deep in its throat!I almost grow weary of testing and debunking official salmon theories.

I imagine that the countless articles (studies) by the ASF indicating that no salmon particles were found in seal stomach content have the same degree of accuracy as those remarks made about salmon not feeding. Go on the Internet and compare the dozens of results of many studies on salmon to those of the ASF, you will be very surprised by the contradictions.

Why in the World are We Waiting?We need to reform the government agencies and the federations and the foundations that control our rivers.We need to get research and real science we can rely on and less bought and paid for propaganda from the East Coast forestry giants.

The Silver Rider originated and tied by the author

The Governor originated and tied by the author

Chapter Three

The Conspiracy

The original title of this book was "EndRun of Atlantic Salmon" it emerged from the "**Enron**" scandal.In a conversation over the phone during the Enron scandal with an old friend Art Lee, I said to Art, "you know, the way the Atlantic salmon establishment and the forest industry are conducting themselves, the boys from Enron don't look that bad after all".Art a master with words mumbled, "ENRON, Enron, enron" . . . And exclaimed . . . "Hey! Pete, how about EndRun of Atlantic Salmon for the title of your book"?I thought the idea was brilliant.

After months of reflection it then dawned on me that "EndRun of Atlantic Salmon" would be oriented toward too much of a limited audience for such a horrendous environmental conspiracy.

****

This chapter will go to the heart of what you need to know about political corruption in Eastern Canada.We must become angry and mobilized if we are to succeed in stopping the larceny and fraud and the deception which is hiding behind the façade of our government regulatory agencies, federations and foundations.In order to become angry and mobilized to reform the current system, we will need to review facts and observe what has now become business as usual in our Natural Resources Industry and understand the motivations and loyalties of the individual decision makers. I will explain this in the best way I can from personal knowledge, based on a half a century of personal observation and exposure to the Atlantic salmon establishment and the logging industry.

****

Since a child I was exposed to the Atlantic salmon environment, having lived year round for an entire life in a salmon lodge located smack in the middle of America's cradle of sport Atlantic salmon fishing.One cannot help but to learn a lot . . . And believe me I did!

The Restigouche River is, in fact, the cradle of Atlantic salmon in North America and from the very beginning the Clubs of the Restigouche River established their dominance as the leaders and controllers of the sport of Atlantic salmon fishing for Canada's East Coast.Starting from this position as a base, and using their unlimited financial resources, they have been able to build a formidable network and extend their controls on government policy, protecting not only their precious private holdings, but also affecting the lives of thousands of people and the economy of an entire region.

I have gathered much of this information from personal contacts, from anglers, administrators of salmon rivers, camp owners, guides, hydrologists, biologists, writers, passionate conservationists, aboriginal people, commercial fishermen, loggers, paper makers, historians, seal hunters, government administrators, chemists, and even from salmon poachers whom many are today excellent guides.

Also from my late uncle John Paul Dubé, was co-coordinator of salmon rivers for the province of Québec, writer, sculpter, Salmon fichera extraordinaire, and passionnate conservationist.J.P., as we called him, was a very close friend, we spent thousands of hours together, fishing, hunting, in conservation programs,meetings and while visiting year round.

Also from my late uncle George Greene, manager of the Hotel Motel Restigouche for three decades, and also manager of the Restigouche Salmon Club for a decade or so.Uncle George enjoyed very much duck hunting, and we spent many hours together in duck blinds.

Also from my late uncle judge André Dubé, lawyer for the Restigouche Salmon Club, an avid salmon angler and hunter. He loved to fish the Matapedia and always stayed at the Hotel Restigouche in the building where he was born.

Also from my uncle Jean Eudes Dubé, federal court judge and former member of Trudeau's cabinet, Jean Eudes was Minister of Publics Works and Minister of Veteran's Affairs for Canada.

Also from Ronald Bujold and the late Clement Gallant who both worked for the Restigouche Salmon Club as office administrators.

1972 The Start of a New Era . . .

Up to 1972 the Atlantic Salmon Association (ASA) worked really hard when **non-riparian directors** were part of the organization bringing back Atlantic salmon to our rivers, and they succeeded in a major "tour de force" in 1972,managing to have all of the commercial salmon nets removed from the Bay des Chaleurs, Newfoundland and Labrador.Our rivers soon became plum full of GIANT salmon.Most anglers fishing during that period could get their limit of two salmon per day just about every day they fished.On the Restigouche the clubs were killing four salmon per day, per club member, as I have mentioned in an earlier chapter.

In 1971 the province of Québec sold approximately eight thousand salmon season licenses annually.By 1974 they were selling over 25,000 annually and the numbers could have continued to grow to three digits if the quality of fishing remained the same for years to come.

History has demonstrated clearly over the years that when a project is accomplished for the benefit of the community, without interference from special interest groups or corruption they can generate unbelievable results.In the early seventies the province of Quebec sold less than ten thousands salmon fishing season licenses as stated above and about the same for moose hunting licenses annually.Moose hunting conservation programs were then oriented to serve the benefit of the Quebec population. Quebec residents were very much involved in establishing the policies and participated in all the conservation programs to increase moose population.This said, the province of Quebec is now selling a **hundred seventy thousand** moose licenses annually, an incredible success.

The Atlantic salmon fishing potential during the mid seventies, had in my opinion, much more potential than moose hunting. Today the province of Quebec is selling as of 2008 about 7,500 **resident** salmon season licenses annually.This is a horrible tragedy evidently allowed by a conspiracy (we will review the sordid details in this chapter) among and between our governments, logging industry and the salmon establishment, who have allowed a handful of super rich individuals to rob us of a national treasure, which are **our** Atlantic salmon and **our** rivers.Really, at the end of the day, this is what it is all about.

Here in 2008 we can see a group of billionaires still acting like feudal lords from the middle ages and nowhere else in North America is the separation of peasantry and nobility more clear than that which is found on the lands and shores of The Restigouche River.Having introduced over a century and a half ago, legal concepts of private property that were already antiquated back then, and corrupting the Provincial governments of Quebec and New Brunswick to award them full ownership of the water rights over many hundreds of miles of vitally important rivers and streams, the Lords of the Restigouche continue to hand these so called "rights" down to successive generations even to this day.Do they really think the people of Quebec and New Brunswick are so ignorant and backward as to not realize when enough is enough?What a corrupt government has given away, an honest government of the people can take back.Our society has rewarded talented and successful business people with wealth and that is the natural goal of most people.Of course it is ok for people to be rich, and ok for them to enjoy their wealth. We are not Bolshevik revolutionaries seeking to take property from the wealthy.However, what the Clubs of the Restigouche call property is not property.Their "rights" are nothing of the sort!**No group of private individuals can own a river that is the life blood of an entire species and then proceed to trap this species all to them-selves in that river.The idea itself is crazy.**The present concept of Riparian Rights is an antique relic and has no place in the modern world where government must manage not only the survival of animal and fish species but also manage the real rights of the general public to access rivers, lakes and streams.After all, these resources, especially Atlantic salmon, have been maintained by government expenditures for the public benefit and for the benefit of the environment.In the old days, at the turn of the 20th century, things were different, there was no government investment in this area and no people either.It is one thing to ask the government for the free use of something that no one else is using, especially if you have to travel for 100 miles across the wilderness to get there and you are self sufficient once you get there.This is not the case anymore, these billionaire freeloaders now come by train, by air, by automobile and road, they have electricity, they have law enforcement protection, they have bridges, they have phones, they have a year round work force, and they have a fish that has so far been protected from extinction.All of this has been provided by government and funded by the people.This has not been done just so a few rich guys can enjoy things all to themselves as their all powerful industrialist predecessors once did.

The next few pages might give you the impression that I am moving away from the above subject. On the contrary, I am building a foundation, an extremely important element that will demonstrate beyond any reasonable doubt, that at the root of the present policies driven by the Atlantic Salmon Federation, one will find the Clubs of the Restigouche River.

The Quiet French Revolution

The following is at the root of most of our salmon policies today . . .

When the first French settlers arrived to America and built communities in Eastern Canada, the Catholic Church had a constant presence in the people's lives and the development of these communities. The poorer and the least educated the people, the more vulnerable they were to be dominated. The Catholic Church capitalized on above facts and established their dominance and control over these French communities. The power of the Catholic Church extended much further than just the limit of these villages; politicians at the Québec National Assembly knew very well to get elected it was a priority to have the Church on their side.

I can clearly remember until my early teens, every evening after supper our family so as all French families in Quebec got on their knees and recited the rosary.The Catholic Priest appointed by the bishop to a village, would every year at times twice a year, visit all the households of his community. The visit consisted of collecting the yearly tithe and also pressuring the woman of the house to remain pregnant at all times, large families were encouraged by the church.The French Quebecquers until the early to mid sixties had one of the highest birth rates in the world.It was very common for French families to have ten or more kids; our local priest father Richard from St-Alexis had twenty-two brothers and or sisters.The Aubé family living in the CNR foreman's house beside the Restigouche Salmon Club had twenty-seven children.

We can see today a similarity between the situation in Israel which has a very low birth rate to that of the Palestinian's who have a very high birth rate.The smaller the families the more money is available for the kids to get educated, while the larger families have to content themselves to a low paying jobs due to lack of education.

French Quebecquers were renowned as very hard working people, dependable, faithful and very honest. Most had large families to feed, thus long intense hours of work was the only way they knew how to survive. The much lower birth rate of English families in Quebec made education affordable, thus in return they were able to obtain the majority of the best paying jobs. It is well known that the French Quebecquers hard labor at low pay made many English families very rich. In this process, which they endured for 2 centuries, many French Quebecquers were so abused to the human limit of hard labor that they were once called the white slaves of America.

In the mid sixties Quebecquers started to free themselves from the influence of the Catholic Church, resulting in birth rates dramatically dropping to one of the lowest in the world today.Education became affordable due to the smaller families and along with this, over time, better paying jobs.Today French Quebecquers are among the most, if not the most, educated people in the country.

The more people are educated the more they are aware of their rights, the more they are aware of their rights, the more demanding they become and the less tolerant they are to abuses.

At the peak of the 2nd French Revolution in Quebec, one could read on the back of Restaurant meal tickets "Québec sait faire" meaning "Quebec knows how", a clear demonstration of the new attitude of French Quebecquers.Now freed from two and a half centuries of total dominance by the English, the French Quebecquers felt confident and now wanted to be **masters of their own province**.

Also for those two and a half centuries hard working French Quebecquers had no time to hunt and fish, thus leaving entire forests and rivers to Americans and English Canadian to grab as their own private clubs.

This brought on many changes and demands from the general public, now that Quebecquer's have the time and the money, **they want to hunt and fish** in their **own** province.Only one barrier limited Quebecquers access to the forests, rivers and lakes and that was the private club-controlled territory, which prevented access.Dismantling of the clubs was required and the bulk of good hunting and fishing areas were leased by the Quebec government to **clubs**.

Frustration among French Quebecquers over a number of issues escalated; the separation of Quebec from Canada was on the front burner; fury from Quebecquers skyrocketed demanding the immediate dismantling of the private "rights" of the **all** hunting and fishing clubs in the province. The separatist party as well as the liberal and the conservative parties, all scrambling to get elected, had no choice but to go with the flow.

As the anti club frustration escalated, a movement emerged in Quebec called the "**De-clubbing movement**" and one can be certain that they were determined to do away with all the private hunting and fishing rights enjoyed by clubs including clubs of the Restigouche River. One could read signs posted on the banks of the Matapedia and Restigouche River; "F......n Yankee Go Home" clearly indicating the clubs were targeted. The Quebec government did not have much choice but to release the entire province leased club territories, lakes and rivers to be transferred to the public.

Collision of Events

Many events were taking place all seemingly at the same time.The Clubs of the Restigouche River were on the brink of losing their grip on the control of the Atlantic Salmon Association which had its headquarters in Montreal.Many non club members and non-riparian owners had managed to become directors of the ASA and were beginning to become involved in decisions and policies of the association.This created serious issues for the riparian owners who were in fear of losing control of their association... a quick move had to be made and we will observe these moves and the resulting consequences shortly.

The French **De-clubbing movement** emerged precisely during the same period as the ban of commercial netting in the Bay des Chaleur, Newfoundland and Labrador by the Atlantic Salmon Association.

Then anti club sentiment propagated to Northern New Brunswick, mainly in the French towns of Kedgwick, Saint Quentin and Saint Jean Baptist. Now that the local residents had had the taste of awesome angling following the lifting of the commercial nets, they wanted more, much more, and were prepared to fight for it.

One hundred years of the clubs total monopoly over the Restigouche River was at stake, and the **de-clubbing movement** tensions escalated to a point where the Restigouche Salmon Club lost all of Red Bank fishing waters and the camp that went with it. And if that was not enough, the local population wanted possession of the rest of the river.

The Clubs of the Restigouche River Under Siege

The clubs of the Restigouche River mainly the Restigouche Salmon Club were all in total panic, afraid of losing their salmon fishing waters, and seeking an urgent solution. So many salmon in the Restigouche River was BAD NEWS for these clubs, as the local anglers wanted to participate in the sport or worse yet open up all the good fishing to the general public.

It did not take much for the clubs of the Restigouche River to figure-out what had gone wrong. Their worst possible nightmare nearly became reality. The phenomenal increase of the salmon runs in the Restigouche River and Eastern Canada, following the lifting of the commercial nets had created a demand for Atlantic salmon fishing by the public and politically, the Quebecquers of the Quiet Revolution were not very sympathetic to the idea of being excluded from fishing by the English speaking billionaires of The Restigouche.

Before the lifting of the commercial fishing nets on the Restigouche River was fair to mediocre, thus not drawing much interest among the local population to fish for salmon. Following the lifting of the commercial nets, the Restigouche River filled-up plumb full of GIANT Atlantic salmon, bringing on a totally different attitude from the local anglers. The word quickly spread that one could catch two GIANT salmon just about every day of fishing. Each year thousands of new resident anglers started to fish for Atlantic salmon, thus increasing the pressure on local anglers to expand their territory.In Quebec during this period the government was dismantling fishing clubs all across the province, and the public kept on demanding even more rivers to be opened up.With this information as background, one can now understand the importance for the clubs of the Restigouche River and their new "alter-ego", The Atlantic Salmon Federation, to find a **quick and permanent solution** if they wanted to hold on to their exclusive fishing waters.

WHO is the Atlantic Salmon Federation?

To start with the Atlantic Salmon Federation **is not** a federation at all in the sense that this implies some kind of public service and public benefit mission. It's really a **Boy's Club**, a VERY tightly controlled sort of private club with a high sounding name but more precisely it is the public relations department for the private **Clubs of the Restigouche River and they have a lot of nerve soliciting the rest of us to send them money for this.**

Some sixty years ago, the Restigouche Salmon Club along with a few other clubs of the Restigouche River formed the Atlantic Salmon Association, which today is the Atlantic Salmon Federation. From the very beginning the Clubs of the Restigouche River mainly the Restigouche Salmon Club had total control of that organization. Today it is a much, much more controlled organization than ever before, under the watchful eyes of the clubs of the Restigouche River. I often make the following comments about the ASF, "it would be much easier to penetrate the CIA in Washington D.C. then it would be to penetrate the ASF", and believe me I'm not far from the truth.

Peter Kaine is a very close friend to the ASF, and an ambassador for the organization. He even has a house in St-Andrews New Brunswick near the ASF headquarters. During a discussion one day I asked Peter "do you know where all the money donated to the ASF is been spent?"His answer "NO, but I am going to St-Andrews next week, I have to go to the ASF office and I will pick up a copy of their spending budget", my answer to Mr. Kaine was good luck! Three weeks later Peter is back at my place of business, during supper after having a few toddies and a bottle or two of wine I thought it would be a good time to ask, "Peter did you manage to get the ASF spending budget?", he answered, "don't ask", admitting they would not give it to me.

During the early seventies guys like Keith Smith and Randy Selki were regular clients at my lodge, both were very much involved with the ASA at its headquarters office in Montreal. (ASA now ASF). These two guys really worked hard supporting the ASA, their strong conviction of ASA role sparked frequent animated arguments with me, especially late in the evenings.Keith and Randy were portraying the ASA as an organization that was no longer controlled by the Clubs of the Restigouche River.They'd say "we are now directors of the ASA, within five years or so we'll have total control of that organization".My answer to them was, you guys are dreaming, there is no way the Clubs of the Restigouche River will let you have control, no way period!The following year Keith and Randy arrived at my place of business, I asked them . . . well boys, what do you think of the ASA moving to St-Andrew's New Brunswick 800 miles away from Montreal?Are you guys going to travel from Montreal to St-Andrews for the ASA meetings?

The move to St-Andrew was unquestionably made entirely to re-gain absolute total control of that organization, and today it would be impossible to penetrate it except for maybe the Federal Taxing Authorities in the US and Canada.

When reading Peter Newman's book "The Canadian Establishment" volume one page 375, one can clearly understand the unprecedented financial and political powers the Clubs of the Restigouche River retain, the Restigouche Salmon Club having the lion's share. The Irving's of Downs Gulch Salmon Club on the Restigouche River, own most of the province of New Brunswick; they have total control over financial and political decisions within that province.

Since the ASA moved to St-Andrew, access to the yearly board meetings where the elections take place are not accessible to most members; it is practically only the executive that can participate if any election at all. This explains why the same group from the Restigouche River is always in control of the ASF.

Now that we understand who REALLY is in charge of Atlantic salmon policies on the East Coast, let's take a closer look at how these people operate . . .

A Plan for Keeping Control of Club Waters . . .

When one observes a couple of decades of environmental crimes and documents these violations and names the violators and then reports this information to the government, one might expect the regulatory agencies to be grateful for any information to help them do their job. Especially if this information is well documented scientifically, with chart measurements and photos. That is except in New Brunswick where violators and the government are virtually one and the same.

This report is following over six months of exchanging correspondences with different departments from the government of New Brunswick, please read the final report sent to the Honourable Premier Shawn Graham . . .

Matapedia August the 29th, 2007.

Government of New Brunswick

The Premier's Office

Centennial Building

P. O. Box 6000

Fredericton, New Brunswick

E3B 5H1

ATTENTION: Hon. Shawn Graham premier of New Brunswick

Dear Mr. Premier:

This is our **Final Report**

Without Prejudice

Please find in the following pages our reply to the New Brunswick Department of Environment and the Department of Natural Resources reports following our demand under the Canada Right to Information Act on spring water yield following clear-cut-logging in the province.

It is very disturbing for us to perceive in these reports that both of your departments have taken the position . . . That removal of forest cover has virtually no effect on spring water yield, while countless studies clearly demonstrate totally the opposite.Instead, they (the departments) blame the whole matter on the results of Climate Change and Global Warming which is, quite properly, an issue of concern.THIS IS MERELY A TACTIC ON THEIR PART, to avoid accountability for their failures to properly regulate the logging industry. This bureaucratic cover-up of decades of environmental abuse, which they have permitted to occur, is easily exposed as you will read in our report.

We believe that public hearings and an independent investigation by the Department of Justice into the inter-actions between the individuals representing private forestry interests and the regulatory departments in the province are absolutely required.We need to understand how these horrendous environmental crimes have been permitted to occur without legal or regulatory proceedings being brought by the government against the private individuals and forestry companies responsible.

Illegal Clear Cut Logging has Occurred, No Doubt About It.We will show the evidence, photography, dates and times, water flow measurements, etc.It is all documented in our report along with some history of inaction and failures by government regulation and enforcement.

For Your Information, here is a brief description on the effects of clear-cut-logging that you and the general public will easily understand:

In a mature evergreen forest snow is intercepted by trees, most of this snow never reaches the ground. Snow captured by trees will evaporate in the atmosphere, this phenomenon is called evaposublimation. It is well documented that up to three times more snow will accumulate on the ground following removal of an evergreen forest in our northern atmosphere.

During the period from Julian day 94 and 115, trees absorb a tremendous amount of water, it is known that a very large maple tree can drink as much as a full barrel of water in one single warm spring day.

In a virgin forest there is a thick moss layer on the ground, this moss is filled with trillions of tiny holes (air spaces) capturing dead air.Dead air is one of man's best known insulation, just like the rock wool in your wall at home, moss insulate the ground and protect it from freezing during the winter. As heavy machinery enters the forest it completely crushes the moss leaving the ground compacted and unprotected from freezing.

Wind speed in clear-cut openings is 2.5 times faster than in the forest, thus snow is transported by wind in the openings, transported snow will harden up and lose its insulation properties.

As spring arrives there is three times more snow on the ground in clear-cut openings than in the virgin forest. Trees that once absorbed a tremendous amount of water each day are now gone.The ground that sponged most of the water is now incapable of absorbing any water as it is frozen. The short rays of the sun in direct contact with the snow in clear-cut openings make the snow melt up to three times faster than in the forest.

Having the ground unprotected from the cover of the trees and moss, it is now frozen solid.Studies have demonstrated that clear-cut openings in an evergreen forest can generate up to 600% increase in spring water yield. The dramatic increase in spring water yield following clear-cut-logging can no longer penetrate the ground; it rushes on the compacted and frozen land surface to the brook, which then becomes engulfed with excessively high water. Creating massive erosion, which one can easily recognize at the mouth of all brooks exposed to clear-cut-logging.

It is not surprising at all when examining Environment Canada's Data water discharge meters for the Restigouche River to confirm the increase of spring water yield following clear-cut-logging. Meter number 01BC001 shows a dramatic water yield increase of 450% in just forty years between Julian day 94 and 115.

This dramatic increase of spring water yield provokes the Restigouche to dump its massive ice much earlier than what nature intended.These gigantic slabs of very thick and powerful ice are propelled down river Tsunami style by the torrent of raising water. Forming massive ice jams that are tearing the riverbanks, channels and pools to shreds. It is only of matter of a few more decades before the Restigouche is in total ruin.

Do you see this picture Mr. Premiere (?) and do you see why this is not even close to being a Global Warming issue (?) and do you understand that man-made events have caused extraordinary damage to our rivers and our Atlantic Salmon habitat.

Our Departments and Agencies are covering up environmental crimes as well as their failure(s) to protect public resources.What are those of us who see this outrageous damage every spring, supposed to do?Are we supposed to just accept financial ruin and thank the Department for its condolences as they blame our loss on Global Warming?In years past, our parents would accept abuses from wealthy industrial owners and their manipulations of government, but those days are now past.We are indignant that our own government departments are so corrupt and so lazy and so out of touch with the facts, as to think that working class people are too ignorant to understand wrongdoing and to investigate matters like this independently.Our Report and our Demands follow herein:

PREAMBLE:

Concerned individuals and environmental groups have been observing and documenting forestry management policies in the province of New Brunswick for many years.The facts resulting from these observations forces us to consider questions concerning the legal duty of certain governmental agencies to enforce environmental laws and regulations and the responsibility of private business(s) to bear the economic consequences of massive environmental abuses.There is no room for even the slightest doubt that the Government of New Brunswick has been, and remains to this day, either unwilling or unable to discipline forest industry practices in this province, despite having a constitutional and legal obligation to act in the public interest.

There is convincing evidence clearly demonstrating that senior officials of certain regulatory agencies place their loyalties with, and receive their instructions from, individuals outside of government.We are unable to detect the exercise of any regulatory functions within these agencies which is an issue we will expose in great detail in this report.We will site normal operating procedures where these agencies are routinely observed operating as a public relations tool of the privately owned forestry giants they are supposed to be regulating.In short, Governmental regulation of the forest industry is totally non-existent in New Brunswick.

As will be shown further herein, the largest forest industry players in New Brunswick are virtually self regulated and totally free to follow their own creative rules and putting private money and profits above all other concerns.This has resulted in massive economic and environmental destruction.Billions of dollars of public resources have been wasted and destroyed already in this province and in the Gaspe region of Quebec as well.This destruction and its root cause(s) are well known to the New Brunswick Department of Natural Resources, and have been documented by scientists within the department and monitored continuously by outside analysts.

Of particular concern to us is the public posturing used by responsible individuals in government to cover up their own embarrassing failures and the extraordinary energy they exert in protecting their corporate handlers.

The global phenomenon of Climate Change is an environmental issue which is clearly a cause for international concern.We recognize the contribution of global warming to the degradation of our ecosystems.No question about it.Nonetheless we will observe how quickly the keepers of the public trust seek to cover up the catastrophic effects of clear cut forest logging by blaming all these effects on global warming and using the public interest in, and fear of, global warming to deflect attention from the crimes of their corporate friends and the government's failure to protect the public from harm and to conserve our precious resources which were once a national treasure.

Certainly, the matters presented herein and which will be further developed in due course, comprise one of the most scandalous political events in the history of Canada.No legal actions have been brought, no sanctions have been ordered, no abuses corrected, no discipline whatsoever, has been brought against the individuals and private corporations responsible for these environmental crimes and horrendous economic losses to the people of eastern Canada.This is not professional incompetence, it is political corruption and we seek to expose the facts of this situation through public hearings and legal actions.

SPECIFIC ISSUES AND FINDINGS:

Massive abuses of forestry practice without adequate control for the past five decades, have had catastrophic consequences on our salmon rivers. Today our salmon rivers are suffering massive erosion problems.Millions of tons of earth which were formerly anchored by aboriginal forests in higher elevations have now become huge silt deposits in the estuaries. Massive erosion deposits have filled most pools in the main river, and it will be creeping into all the tributaries of the basin in the next few decades. Severely deteriorated salmon habitats are made even worse by dramatic incidents of ice scouring, and over four-fold increases (above normal) of spring water runoff (yield), and devastating low water flows during summer.

Our salmon rivers are about one third wider then just fifty years ago, about half as deep, and contain half the water flow during the summer.Water temperatures in summer on the Restigouche and other rivers like the Miramichi have exceeded 81F.Micro-organism populations, unheard of in these rivers in the past, are now exploding in this warm soup, diseases are spreading like wild fire, and salmon are dying by the thousands each year.These rivers, once the most prolific habitat of the Atlantic salmon in the world, are not even a shadow of their former selves.This destruction is entirely man made and a phenomenal public resource has been sacrificed for the economic profits of a few individuals.Our great salmon rivers are on the edge of total ruin and will soon be useless for public fishing.It can now only be a matter of a short time. This situation has been brought on almost entirely by clear-cut-logging practices.The Provincial Government of New Brunswick cannot deny that a hideous abuse of the environment has occurred.

We must allow no excuses and make no mistakes in understanding the main issues, causes and effects here.We have lost many opportunities and chances to save the rivers already.We have trusted a government who has abused this trust by turning over their responsibility for research and "fact finding" to certain private foundations that are also under control of the forestry industry.Good science and conservation efforts have been subverted by organizations and foundations that operate quietly under the control of those same individuals and corporations whose highly destructive (and profitable) forestry practices have caused almost all our problems.They seek to use the cover of these foundations as a smoke screen to produce false findings and pseudo science to cover up the real problems facing our rivers.

The executives of private industry and the management executives of the foundations they control, and members of government are seen "working" (and playing) hand in hand together, as they occupy the best pools on our best rivers in total privacy.Government agencies have been remiss in their responsibility by deferring to this unholy alliance; particularly those individuals who have received handouts and private privileges.Many of those in positions of governmental authority operate under a system of policies corrupted by the very industry they are supposed to regulate. Through laziness, apathy, and corruption, they are also happy to use industry controlled "science" and promote industry propaganda.We can expect no other results than what we have experienced. The status quo cannot be allowed to continue and all of these individuals must be removed from positions of responsibility.

How in the world can the government of New Brunswick explain how they have allowed such a disaster to happen to the world's most beautiful and productive salmon rivers?Is it possible that the New Brunswick government was that incompetent?Answer:No!There are many excellently qualified individuals in government who know the facts but lack the authority to act and others who do have the authority but are afraid to use it.The loyalty of others, sadly, appears to have been bought off.Is it possible that the New Brunswick government was that grossly negligent?Answer:Yes, this much at least is clear.What is even clearer however, is that the New Brunswick government was, and still remains, intimidated by the eastern giants of Canada's forest and paper industry; some of whom have previously used heavy handed tactics with the CBC with much success.

The most obvious answer and of course the most troubling, is corruption within the government itself.Corruption can take many forms, and some of these forms, may be entirely legal under Canadian law.Nonetheless, legal or otherwise, the Department of Natural Resources of New Brunswick operates no differently than if it were under private control by industry which all evidence indicates that it is.This evidence shows that private corporations have been given a "defacto license" to waste public resources to facilitate private profits; a license that has allowed them to operate without proper supervision for decades, comfortable in the knowledge that their shameful forestry practices would not be challenged.There are also troubling questions about personal wealth and under the table compensation for those in position of authority which must be addressed along with a list grievances, claims, and losses by property owners and business enterprises that have long been ignored by their own government.

Whatever the reason or reasons, it is hard to believe that the leaders from the New Brunswick government did not detect the presence of the logging and paper industry executives who infiltrated the Atlantic Salmon Federation to gain control, not only of the management of that foundation, but also the privilege of working with government to establish policies and regulations affecting our salmon rivers.

Thousands of anglers depended on and supported the Atlantic Salmon Federation, thinking it would be helping to protect their salmon rivers.It certainly does not seem to be the case here today.Our salmon runs are on the brink of extinction; the structures of our salmon rivers are falling apart; the food chain in the North Atlantic is out of whack with voracious salmon predators such as seals and cormorants totally protected and thus out of control.Why would a supposedly independent "science" based foundation just ignore these impacts on salmon populations?How in the world did the government of New Brunswick allow all these events to happen?

Salmon anglers have been in the dark since the beginning of these problems in Canada.They know that the fishing has deteriorated but do not know why.They have contributed billions to Foundations and to the Canadian economy, but the vast majority of these individuals do not live here and in fact reside in population centers hundreds and even thousands of miles away from the salmon rivers.They do not see, year after year, decade after decade, what we, who live on the rivers see.

Clear evidence shows that certain groups have gained generously from the deterioration of our salmon rivers, particularly the logging industry.A depressed sport fishery is the right climate for them.It creates fewer first hand observers and results in less complaints to government from witnesses objecting to the slaughtering of the New Brunswick forest and the obvious effects on the fishing waters.

Also, let us not forget the riparian owners who struggled to save their private fishing waters during the mid-seventies.During that period a de-clubbing movement led by the 2nd French revolution in Quebec, was out to dismantle all clubs within its province, this movement also spread to northern New Brunswick.In 1976 the Restigouche Salmon Club lost all of its Red Bank fishing waters, the riparian owners of the Restigouche River were then under siege and a quick solution was required to save their fishing waters.We do not need to point out to anyone who these private owners are.

Dramatically decreasing salmon runs in the Restigouche River and other rivers in the province of New Brunswick could greatly benefit the logging industry and the riparian owners who are virtually one and the same.If the fishing could be rendered marginal, then the growing demand by the public to open up all waters to the public could be blunted.Stopping the government movement toward granting public access to their private fishing pools, even on a limited basis, became the paramount objective for these people.For the past century, at least, legal ownership of these private waters has been considered one of the sacred privileges of the upper class and sharing this resource in any manner with the public is totally unthinkable to them.The incredible irony of this is the fact that not one penny of taxes are paid by the wealthy elite on these properties even though the fair market value on these properties is in the millions of dollars.Apparently only ordinary people are required to pay taxes on property.One could also cite the huge subsidy(s) paid on behalf of these private owners by the government in the form of employment insurance benefits for their workers. Apparently it is a crucial priority that ordinary people be taxed so the government can use these funds to pay for over half the annual cost of those seasonal workers who are indispensable to insuringthat these wealthy owners and their guests may be pampered in luxury and comfort.We grow tired of making lists and showing examples of this kind of unfairness.We return to our main discussion on the subject of corruption:

Two issues were conveniently presented by the powerful owners and the foundations with perfect timing to insure major cooperation in their objective to preserve Salmon fishing for themselves, and to restrict opportunities for Salmon fishing by the less worthy general public.These issues are Seal Hunting and The Aboriginal fishery for Atlantic salmon.Stopping the century old practice of Arctic seal hunting would decrease salmon numbers by allowing a dramatic increase in the numbers of these prolific salmon predators.Also it is a well established fact that the Aboriginals never used gill nets prior to 1973.Soon after the ban on commercial gill net fishing for Atlantic salmon in 1972, the Aboriginal started blocking the mouth of our salmon rivers.

Having personally worked while acting as president of the Société d'opération des rivières Matapedia et Restigouche (S.O.R.M.E.R.) with Mr. Wilfred Carter then president of the ASF, it did not take me too long to figure out what was going on. There was very little if at all no incentive from Mr. Carter to have the Aboriginal fishery stopped.

These reduced salmon runs were the key that would allow the Atlantic Salmon Federation, which was already by then nothing but a mouthpiece for the very secretive and highly private Restigouche River Salmon Clubs, to introduce Catch & Release regulations to the government as a "science based" policy.The private parties behind these regulations could hide behind the actions of government.

One is amazed to observe how quickly and easily the government adopted all the policies proposed by the private owners! (In reality it was very well known that these regulations would result in a reduction of over 80% of the Salmon fishing license applications and completely eliminate the movement to open the private waters of the Restigouche to the public.)Introducing Catch & Release required a salmon population that could arguably be considered an endangered species.As the goal of reducing the salmon populations was obtained, the introduction of Catch & Release rules was then a piece of cake to have enacted as the rule of law.After the introduction of Catch & Release the **resident** salmon anglers would quit salmon fishing, leaving entire rivers to the private riparian owners, and the logging industry to slaughter our forest with little or no intervention from the public.

Canada is at bottom of OECD reports the Simon Fraser Institute.Canada with one of the world's worst environmental records, occupies the twenty-eighth position out of the 30 most industrialized countries of the world. New Brunswick and Quebec have one of the world's worst forestry management programs.The province of Quebec with merely 4.8% of its land surface as protected zones and New Brunswick providing not much more, look poor in comparison to the US when considering that the US has 10 times the population density of Canada, while still managing to protect 25% of its land surface as protected zones.

What concerns our group is the fact that we are the victims of these massive abuses from totally out of control deforestation programs.Thousands of people in Eastern Canada have lost jobs, and many more will be lost in the near future.We, the victims, have all been failed by government.We and our sportsman clients have made billion of dollars of investments in this salmon fishery.Other workers have invested heavily in their logging equipment, in small saw mills; many have invested generations of their lives working in paper mills and the lumber trade.Forests are a renewable resource, but it will take several generations for these devastated forests to be renewed and when they are renewed they will contain only the most profitable wood species, and will lack the biodiversity of the former forests.Meantime, the billionaire landowners have banked decades of profits while the workers who cannot afford long layoffs, lose homes and equipment to bank foreclosures.All of these results have been engineered by managers setting in corporate offices, many of them have no other job other than manipulating the controls on the machinery of government.The modern corporation is an artificial creature, licensed by government, with no conscience, and whose entire objective is to consume capital and to turn this capital into profits and more capital.When this creature is also allowed to control its own government oversight agency(s) we have created a virtually indestructible monster.

There is a good reason why, in all civilized countries, there is a solid wall between Public and Private interest. Without it you get what we have experienced here in Eastern Canada; private inurement at public expense.

A few of our more famous Canadian billionaires have a horrible record of destroying the environment.The almost forgotten incident of The Irving Whale is just one outrageous example; demonstrating the Government's lack of interest and ability to enforce environmental laws and regulations.In retrospect we have every right to question how easily the Irving Company was able to avoid responsibility in the careless shipment of this dangerous cargo which resulted in the release of thousands of tons of contamination in the Gulf of St. Lawrence.Even today some of the most toxic substances on earth continue to leech from the site into the Gulf.It is absurd how totally unprotected we are here in Canada from even this most horrendous of environmental crimes.The Irving Company refused to take responsibility even though much of the evidence indicated that negligence played a role in this disaster. The Canadian taxpayers were left to foot hundreds of millions of dollars in clean up costs. Even though as one of Canada's shipping giants, one presumes that The Irving Company was insured against losses. This disaster was easily, by any measure of environmental disasters, on a similar level as the Exxon Valdez oil spill in AlaskaYet, compare the action of US government regulatory agencies and prosecutions against Exxon Mobil in the US Federal and Alaska State Courts with the chumminess of our government regulators with The Irving Company and you see something that is so absurd as to defy all reason.Exxon Mobile was required to pay many billions of dollars in compensation for losses and damages to private and public resources.The Irving Company, arguably one of the richest private companies in Canada, is able to walk away free and clear from a disastrous debacle.We can assume with absolute confidence that there is massive political corruption protecting The Irving Company's private interests here in Eastern Canada.There can be no other explanation. This is just one of several relationships with our government agencies that we have been investigating in connection with the irreparable harm to our public resources.

With control of the government machinery and the media in the hands of such powerful people we expect a hard fight here in Canada.It is clear, and easily demonstrated, that the government(s) here are not following their own laws and regulations so we will start with those facts.Despite the sophistication of many of our Canadian Social Systems, we are remarkably third world and parochial when it comes to legal matters involving collection of tax revenues, regulating large corporations, and protecting our natural resources.Certain private interests have taken advantage of our system of government.We are not a people who derive from a long history of government prosecutions against big business tycoons and industrial abuses.We are proud to be an honest and generous and caring people but we will not suffer corruption to follow us and our children into this century like we did during the last.We have long detested the litigious and antagonistic business attitudes of our American brothers to the south as well as the frequent adversarial nature of their government regulatory agencies toward business.We do not wish to introduce this way of life into Canada but since our own government agencies continue to deny obvious violations of law and regulation even when given solid evidence, we have no choice other than to seek help where we can get it.

It is our intention to bring this evidence before Federal courts of law in competent jurisdictions in both Canada and in The United States of America.Clearly there have been violations of not only Canadian Law but also violations of International Law and United States Laws.The US in particular has two laws pertaining to crimes and the subversion of justice in other countries that serve benefits for their investments in the US.Two of these laws are: the US Prohibited Foreign Corrupt Practice Act and the US Alien Tort Claims Act.The shame of this for Canada, is the fact that these laws were largely intended to prevent the corruption of third world governments by large corporations.It is outrageous that we are forced to this juncture over the private fishing pools of a few tycoons in New Brunswick.

Our group has contacted law firms, in US states not controlled by the forest industry, with the objective to prosecute the corporate titans who have ruled the province of New Brunswick for the last half century. Our economic model justifies claims and monetary damages and possible punitive damages in excess of $20 billion (CND) on behalf of the people of New Brunswick and Gaspe, Quebec.If necessary our legal complaints can be filed in US federal Court at any time.

However we have a better solution for all concerned:We are demanding public hearings here in Eastern Canada.In these public forums the people will speak and deliver information publicly that has only been discussed with us privately in the past. (Those who speak out are individuals with firsthand knowledge of secret deals and destructive events that have been ignored by the government and which constitute violations of law and regulations).Canadian law is sufficient to prosecute political corruption and corporate wrongdoing.One way or another, this train is leaving the station.We demand access to our government officials and public accountability in front of mainstream Canadian media.

To prepare this media for what is to come, I have written a book . . . "Endrun of Atlantic Salmon" which is scheduled to be published in the US, Canada and Europe. The Endrun word came to mind during the Enron scandal, which is an appropriate title for the situation.We expect Endrun of Atlantic Salmon to generate horrendous publicity with worldwide media attention.Salmon anglers, especially **residents** of New Brunswick who will read this book will be accurately informed, and in a much better position to do what we believe should have been done three decades ago.

The above confrontation was brought on due to governmental indifference and/or in-action to compensate those who have been greatly affected by these issues: The **resident** living, and who operate business, on the Restigouche and other salmon rivers in your province, which are suffering immense financial loses due to poor salmon returns. We cannot fail to mention those who have had their business or home destroyed by ice floods in the spring due to dramatic water yield increase from clear-cut-logging. The New Brunswick Government for decades has ignored these manmade events affecting the population, choosing instead to deny that massive clear-cut logging has totally wrecked our Salmon Industry.They acknowledge the results however and do not argue the damages to the environment that we point out.They offer only their bureaucratic condolences for the effects of Climate Change and Global Warming.In other words they seem relieved to have another convenient excuse for doing absolutely nothing.We are challenging this lazy, do nothing, negligence on the part of our Government agencies which serves only to cover up their failures to enforce environmental regulations.Even worse is the fact that these agencies continue to operate like a brothel.They obviously have no moral standards at all when it comes to handing out private favors to wealthy individuals and corporate interests in violation of the public trust.

Our demands are simple and non-negotiable except possibly for the timing of certain events: Public hearings addressing these matters must be announced and advertised by the appropriate government agency(s) within the next 2 months and these hearings must be scheduled for a date certain which must be reasonably soon thereafter.We are willing to abide by the outcome of these hearings as we have no doubt that they will result in appropriate action by the Federal Justice System here in Canada.

It is entirely appropriate for aggrieved citizens to petition the government in matters like this and entirely unacceptable for the government to ignore or refuse such a reasonable demand as to hold and preside over public hearings.Failure to hold these hearings will necessitate the filing of formal complaints in other Courts of Law, as discussed earlier, and which is odious to us and an embarrassment to Canada."We stand on guard for thee".

Sincerely yours,

Pete Dubé

Motel Restigouche Outfitters

5 rue des Saumons

Matapedia, Quebec

G0J 1V0

Copy to:

The Minister of Environment

The Minister of Natural Resources

Mr. Bill Taylor Atlantic Salmon Federation

Ms. Nelda Craig Environment Water Science

Ms. Gail Darby RTI Coordinator

Answer from Premier Shawn Graham

In Premier Shawn Graham's answer, Mr. Graham's acknowledges that Northern New Brunswick snow pack accumulations have **decreased** by 25% in the last 30 years. In his own words: "It should also be noted that the snow pack in northern New Brunswick has decreased by 25% over the last 30 years".

The Honorable Premier's above (comment) is a dead giveaway, how can he now explain Environment Canada's dramatic spring water yield increases records of up to 450% on the upper Restigouche and the same for most rivers in New Brunswick if there is 25% less snow accumulations during the winter?Less snow equals obviously less water yield, should it not Messr. the Premier?It's clear . . . massive deforestation is the culprit behind massive water yield increases, period!

I just hope the people of New Brunswick will now see through the smoke screen set up by their government, hiding from the public the facts that their shameful forests programs have totally devastated our echo systems. Out of control logging is today directly responsible for water flooding in Quebec and New Brunswick, even Riviére au Renard in the Gaspé during the summer of 2007 would have had maybe up to seventy percent less damage if logging in that area had been done responsibly.

Imagine the Capital City of New Brunswick "Fredericton", where the New Brunswick parliament sits, after all the City's Motto is: Fredericopolis silvae filia nobilis. (Fredericton noble daughter of the forest)

The bottom line is Mr. the Premier . . . the noble daughter of the forest was and is still being raped in every-which-way one can imagine, only a few rags are now covering her scarred naked body from four decades of shameful logging abuses.The Nobel Daughter of the Forest is now drawing attention, reminding the city of Fredericton where the laws to abuse her have been manipulated, she is now making front-page news: "the city of Fredericton is underwater", those who are responsible for having raped her are now getting their feet wet. Flooding during the spring of 2008 in New Brunswick and Quebec is directly the cause of massive deforestation programs, climate change has absolutely nothing to do with these flooding events, since there were no unusual climate events or excessive rain fall, we now know who's responsible for it.

Nothing will be done by petitioning the government of New Brunswick, that much is clear. They will not even address the charges, choosing instead to deflect the problems on to global warming or offering a lame brush off quoting the wonderful environmental laws that New Brunswick has on the books.I already knew the laws were there, my only question was, here are the violations and the violators, are you going to enforce the laws or not!Apparently the answer is not.This is itself a violation of the law!Litigation and public outrage are just around the corner.The people of New Brunswick are victims of massive political corruption by the logging industry and this conspiracy must be exposed and ended.

Setting the stage:

Acquiring complete control of our forest and rivers was not something the giant logging companies accomplished overnight.There was a steady series of events, over several decades which resulted in the governments of two provinces being corrupted.The deputy ministers for both departments of Natural Resources had to be part of the conspiracy, as well as the people appointed to influential positions for the protection of our echo systems; the Atlantic Salmon Federation, the Quebec Salmon Federation, and the Fondation de la Faune du Quebec, etc. etc.Once all of these organizations were under control, and everyone who participated knew their roles, most especially their LIMITATIONS on authority, the stage was set for a massive system of reward and punishments as we will see.

First, moving the Atlantic Salmon Association to St-Andrews New Brunswick, flushed down the toilet all of the non-riparian owners who were acting as directors for the ASA in Quebec, allowing the clubs and the forestry interests to regain control of that organization.

Secondly, once the ASA was established in St-Andrews New Brunswick, they joined force with the very powerful logging industry; the Irvings; the Frasers; the Rolands; just to name a few . . .

Thirdly, in Quebec, the former Minister du Loisir de la Chasse et de la Pêche, the honorable Guy Chevrette, after leaving the Ministére des Loisires de la Chasse et de la Pêche, became Minister of Natural Resources for the Province of Quebec. Shortly after Le Ministére des Loisires de la Chasse et de la Pêche disappeared **from the map, and fish and game management responsibilities were transferred to the Natural Resources of Quebec.In other words:**"the hen-house was given to the fox to manage", **Quebec was now perfectly set-up with all powers and controls vested in the Department of Natural Resources and there was no higher government oversight of their activities.**

Fourthly, the Quebec Salmon Federation under the influence, if not the total control, of Monsieur Yvon Côté, who was a biologist in charge for the pronvince of Quebec for decades regarding Atlantic Salmon conservation policies and programs. Mr. Côté was very active with the Fédération Québéquoise du Saumons de l'Atlantic (F.Q.S.A.) at the time and even continues in that position today.I believe Mr. Côté did all that was asked and expected to promote and protect the logging company interests and the private rights of the clubs including support for the ASF's plans to reduce salmon stocks.There is more to come on Monsieur Côté later.

We have previously discussed the sudden and dramatic increase in the enthusiasm by the general public for Salmon fishing following the resurgence of fish after the nets were removed.We also discussed the threat this posed to the concept of private fishing rights.

The most effective way the clubs of the Restigouche River had for holding on to its fishing waters rights at the time, was to take steps to drastically decrease the salmon runs as quickly as possible. A huge drop in the salmon runs of the Restigouche River and Eastern Canadian rivers would allow the Atlantic Salmon Federation (the aforementioned boys club) to propose Catch and Release regulations.Once these regulations were introduced as law, it was well known that the vast majority of resident anglers would quit fishing and the clubs would then retain complete control of their private fishing waters for as long as the salmon runs remained low.Let us not forget one very important fact.Low salmon runs do not affect the fishing quality on the prime holding pools of the Restigouche River as these private pools are always holding large numbers of fish even during periods when salmon runs are very low everywhere else.

In the fall of 1973 for **unexplained reasons** the government announced it was stopping the annual seal hunt on Canada's East Coast as of spring of 1974. Following the stop of the seal hunt, numerous articles appeared in the ASF Journal, stating studies by the ASF and or others have demonstrated that seals do not eat salmon. The anglers that are informed know that is totally untrue . . .

Why then did the ASF take such a **strong stand** to protect the seals, if it was not to keep salmon population down?

I believe the seal hunt was stopped by our government for multiple reasons.

First, the Canadian government had the responsibility of protecting the public as the Gulf of St-Lawrence had just been seriously contaminated from an horrendous spill disaster of 7.2 tons of PCB's, released in the Gulf of St-Lawrence by the sinking of the Irving Whale.Obviously much of the cod population was seriously contaminated with PCB's, thus not suitable for public consumption. Environmentalist should not look any further as to why the Beluga's of the St-Lawrence were dying.The seal hunt became a diversion; protecting the Irving Company and allowing it to evade its responsibilities. By the same token these steps resulted in dramatically reducing the cod population and the collapse of the cod fisheries of Atlantic Canada would follow. Once Canada's Atlantic Coast Cod Fisheries collapsed and they were no longer harvesting contaminated cod to be sold to the public, and the case and the problem were solved.

Secondly, the logging industry was able to operate freely even using their worst practices to destroy our salmon rivers.Forget any possibility of interventions form the Foundations and/or the Federations who had the responsibility to protect these rivers.They were already part and parcel of the conspiracy with the government regulators, the loggers and the Riparian owners.

Thirdly, at the bottom of all this, are the riparian owners and the clubs who wanted to conserve for themselves their little private paradise on our best salmon rivers.

On the other hand the most successful salmon conservation organization on the globe"The North Atlantic Salmon Funds" who are having overwhelming success bringing good runs of salmon back to the Irish, Scottish, Norwegians and especially their Icelandic Rivers.Since 2005 Iceland has had its best salmon seasons in their history.Irish, Scottish and Norwegians salmon Rivers are doing very well to say the least. What in the world is wrong here in Canada that our salmon runs are down to nothing, if it's not the policies being promoted by the ASF and their cronies in the government.We know who the ASF is by now ok.It's time to stop the charade!

The North Atlantic Salmon Funds conservation organization out of Reykjavik Iceland strongly believes that seals are at the root of our salmon decline.In the diagram on next page it shows a seal population in the North Atlantic of 11,700,000 seals as of 1998.It is more than possible the seal population has now surpassed the 20,000,000 strong in the North Atlantic.

On the following page a diagram showing (as of 1998) the situation of the North Atlantic ecosystem produced by the North Atlantic Salmon Funds, a world leading salmon conservation organization. Orri Vigfurson of the NASF from Iceland is in my opinion the world foremost and outstanding Atlantic salmon conservation leader.

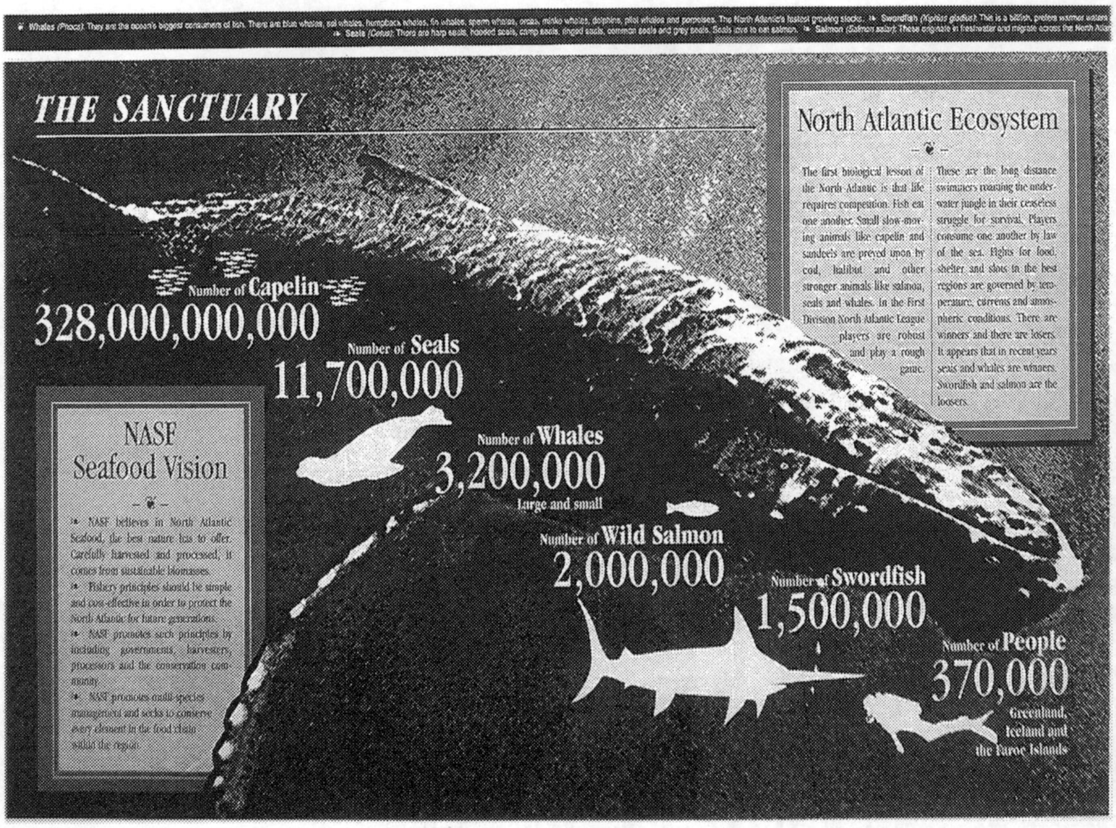

DFO's scientists reports that seal populations have **doubled since 1998**, but, now have **stabilized due to birth rate dropping by some 70% in recent years.**

The year after the lifting of the commercial nets, the Aboriginal who had never fished with gill nets prior to 1972, were now laying gill nets in the estuary of the Restigouche River.By 1978 they were blocking most of the entrance of the river, the salmon runs of the Restigouche dropped dramatically.As I have mentioned in a previous chapter I worked with Wilfred Carter then president of the ASF to have the Aboriginal fishery stopped. It eventually dawned on me that he had no incentive to stop the Aboriginal fishery. The private pools on the Restigouche still had all the salmon his bosses could ever hope to catch.I was kind of suspicious at the time when working with Mr. Carter that something was wrong, but today with my years of observation of the ASF it would not surprise me one bit if (at that time) they cast a blind eye on the Aboriginal Fisheries or even sanctioned these practices behind the scenes just to get the salmon runs down quickly and get the Catch and Release regulations introduced.

It is clear that the ASF is infiltrated by the logging industry, the Irving's, the Fraser's, the Roland's just to name a few.These are the Companies that destroyed the habitat of most of our salmon rivers in Eastern Canada.As described earlier, even the Restigouche Salmon Club joined in the clear-cut-logging frenzy over thousands of acres of virgin forest? I can't believe the RSC did not know that it would ultimately have severe effects on their own salmon fishing pools. Do not forget the outrageous lie told by Al Carter while he was manager of the Restigouche Salmon Club, during the interview by Phil Lee, he had no problem representing that his club was not involved in clear-cutting of its land while totally the opposite was happening.

Clearly, one of the most evil men in the history of the USA is Mr. Joseph Cullman the 3rd, owner of The Philip Morris Tobacco Company.He held, for the longest period of time, the position of chairman of the board of the ASF of any chairman. When Mr. Cullman died in 2004, the ASF could not hold back from glorifying this man, elevating him to the very top of the pedestal as a gentleman a champion conservationist and a wonderful generous kind man.The hypocrisy of this eulogy is above and beyond the usual kind words we expect for the recently departed. Will we speak about the wonderful life and accomplishments of Mr. Charles Manson after he dies in prison?

Mr. Cullman knew for decades, following numerous studies by his company of the devastating health effect tobacco had on humans.Not content with the billions he had already accumulated with the sales of his poisonous cigarettes; Mr. Cullman pushed his chemists day in and day out to develop the most potent cigarettes possible; cunningly increasing the nicotine content of his cigarettes; so the users would become addicted for life.This man had absolutely not the slightest respect whatsoever for the lives of human beings. He was possessed by profit and power at any cost, no matter if it destroyed people's lives. To my experience if one is part of a group especially if the group elects him to the highest position of that group, it's evident to me that the saying "Bird's of a Feather Flock Together" is very appropriate here.Judge people by the company they keep because they are sure to share the same values with one another.

The ASF has also glorified and made a hero out of Lee Wolf, the man with a strong passion for catching twenty-pound plus salmon on a four pound test leader with a number sixteen fly. Mr. Wolf played hundreds of large fish with that "Mickey Mouse equipment", at times for up to three hours and even more. Then releasing these poor traumatized fish, totally exhausted, floating away like a limp rag just to die later (even bragging about Catch and Release). To me this style of fishing for large salmon has to be the most inhumane and unsportsman way to fish for Atlantic salmon, period!

ASF should be promoting totally the opposite, the use of large barbless hook **flies and the quick play and release of fish. It always puzzled me why the ASF never made the use of barbless hooks a policy, and never demanded for a** legal releasing limit with very strict fine.**Anglers can legally release as many salmon as they please, there are no** legal **limits.Strict limits should be mandatory just like** very strict limits **are mandatory for the killing of salmon in Quebec. Why is the use of sinking fly lines during low water permitted when numerous fish are snagged and fowl hooked and killed; why no legal limit on catch and release; why no barbless hooks for catch and release; why allow the presence of thousands of cormorants and mergansers praying on our young salmon; why the massive seal protection programs.**

I have to give credit where credit is due, there is no question that the ASF has done an extraordinary job for the Clubs of the Restigouche River. They have managed to keep salmon anglers in the dark for over three decades while working tirelessly for the clubs to retain full control of their private fishing waters. Their policies are now indistinguishable from those of the Quebec Salmon Federation (FQSA).Mr.Yvon Côté, the president of the FQSA is eating right out of the hand of the ASF and the logging industry.Mr. Côté is drawing ennormous personal benefits from his associations with these powerfull people.From his position of power and influence, he now owns a dream outfitting paradise in the headwaters of the Restigouche on the Kedgwick River.Mr. Côté occupies a 196 square kilometres territory; with 350 square kilometres of exclusive rights for moose and bear hunting; lakes for trout fishing; exclusive rights for salmon fishing on the Kedgwick; four moose hunting seasons. These are **extraordinary rights** worth many millions of dollars in annual income.

How in the world did Mr. Côté, a servant of the public, manage to accumulate such unbelievable privileges.The certain conflicts of interest and the appearance of corruption are so strong here that Mr. Cote should voluntarily come public and explain his good fortune.Only in Eastern Canada would newspaper editors refuse to investigate these facts.I hate to leave such a juicy story as this, but we have more ground to cover.

I was unable to find another logical explanation as to **why the seal hunt was stopped**. Everything indicates, considering the exact timing that the seal hunt was banned, that the only beneficiaries of this ban were the clubs of the Restigouche River who retained total control of their private fishing waters, especially when considering that just about all other fishing clubs in the Province of Quebec were dismantled.

When searching the Internet one can find compelling scientific evidence showing results totally the opposite of those published by the ASF concerning seals and fish farming.All evidence concludes that the ASF "the club's of the Restigouche River" love it the way it is. Small runs of Atlantic salmon are required if Catch and Release is to remain the rule of law for Atlantic Canada.Don't get me wrong now . . . the ASF will not let Atlantic salmon disappear, keeping salmon returns at the current low level remains the goal. Low salmon returns is for the ASF and "the club's of the Restigouche River" the key for holding on to their private salmon fishing rights and to remove incentives for the public to enter the sport.Even in periods of low salmon runs, they will always have more than adequate numbers of salmon for their sport fishing as whatever fish are in the river will migrate to, and hold in, the private waters owned by the clubs.

On average, a mature seal needs about twenty to thirty pounds of fish per day to survive, so one might think that the average seal kills twenty to thirty pounds of fish per day.It would be nice if that was the case, but that is not how it works at all. Seals are extremely bad predators, literally destroying their food supply by wasting most of their kills.Seals will attack their pray from underneath taking one bite out of the stomach of the fish, which includes the liver and the content of the stomach, the richest food value part of the fish.The balance of the fish sinks to the bottom of the ocean.These feeding patterns are very well documented.

The Newfoundland government made a documentary report on the extreme impact of seals on its cod population. This documentary video was aired on National TV, were scuba divers filmed the ocean floor showing thousands of dead cod with one seal bite through the stomach. It is well known among Newfoundland commercial fishermen that seals are the cause of the dramatic decline of the cod stocks, however they were mislead by governments, the media and the ASF into believing that only the lunatic fringes of the animal rights and environmentalist movements are behind the laws and propaganda that is preventing them from continuing their traditional seal hunts.

It is sad, really sad how far greed can push some people to the extreme for personal gain and power. Stopping the seal hunt on Canada's East Coast was a devastating blow to all of the fishing industry.Thousands upon thousands of people, including commercial cod fishermen, processing factories, salmon guides, anglers, inn-keepers, from Newfoundland, Labrador, Nova Scotia, PEI, New Brunswick, Madeleine Islands, and Quebec who have lost their jobs, are now having to expatriate to faraway places for work to survive.

Another fact that is scientifically well documented is this.Seals after having consumed enormous amount of food will spread their excrements throughout their feeding ground, contaminating the entire food chain mainly cod.The ASF is desperately trying to point and find ways to blame the fish farms for the spreading of diseases, but here again not a single word on seals contaminating our fish stocks.

Atlantic Coast Cods and other species are now full of worms and other diseases contacted by seal droppings, and again this is not important for the ASF.

The economic benefits from large runs of salmon in Canada's Atlantic Coast rivers would have created a strong protectionist environment to protect this economic windfall for the benefit of the public. Businesses profiting from the sport fishery and happy anglers would find a strong incentive to stop any activities (out of control clear-cut-logging) that could possibly damage their resource.I very strongly believe the ASF, (riparian owners) and the logging industry were very well aware of above facts.They took matters in their own hands and did what was required to succeed at the expense of the public. They were well aware of the fact that if rivers were plumb full of salmon they would find very strong oppositions to their clear-cut-logging practices. If profit was to come first for the logging industry, it certainly made sense that the less outside people clamoring for the rights to participate in a profitable salmon ecology the better.With the seal hunting ban causing less salmon and thus less clamor for water rights by the public there is less opportunity and desire to confront the logging industry with its environmental crimes. In other words, the ban on seal hunting is in the perverted best interest of the logging industry.

While talking with Newfoundland seal hunters to my surprise I was informed of the following . . . Years ago when Newfoundland seal hunters shot and killed seals in water, those seal could be retrieved a half hour later or longer.Today seals killed in water have to be retrieved immediately or they will sink underwater.Puzzled I asked . . . Why? Why would it not sink before and it's sinking today? . .They have very little blubber left on their body, no more fat for keeping them afloat; they are starving to death, having decimated the fish stocks that they (the seals) and humans must share for survival!Think about this!

How much longer will Canada's Atlantic Coast residents accept to lose billions of dollars in revenue for their region annually, and tens of thousands of lost jobs? What will it take to stop a handful of billionaires from the Restigouche River and radical environmentalists from generating such ill-be-gotten gains arising from the seal hunting conflict?In the next chapter I will enumerate a plan to generate unbelievable economic growth for Eastern Canada and Northern United States.

The Saga of the Sinking and Raising of the Irving Whale

On Tuesday, September 8, 1970, the front page headline of The Chronicle-Harold, Halifax, Nova Scotia daily newspaper, read:

"Oil Barge Goes Down in Gulf With Cargo"

(Above article can be found on the Internet)

The Irving Whale oil tanker sunk on September 7, 1970, in the Gulf of St-Lawrence while en-route from Halifax, Nova Scotia to Bathurst New Brunswick with 4200 tons of Bunker "C" heavy fuel oil and 7.2 tonnes of polychlorinated biphenyl (PCB's).The Irving Whale was built in 1966 at the Saint John Shipbuilding & Dry Dock Co. Ltd. for J. D. Irving Limited in Saint John, New Brunswick.

The tanker lies at the bottom of the Gulf of St-Lawrence about 60 km Northwest of North Point, Prince Edward Island and 100 km Southwest of the Iles-de-la-Madeleine and it is slowly releasing its oil cargo and PCB's in the Gulf of St-Lawrence. The Irving Whale was also accounted for a 13,650 litres oil spill off Newfoundland's Burin Peninsula in February of 1970.

Reports confirmed doors that should have been kept shut were open and, coupled with high seas, resulted in the Irving Whale being swamped. It appears that negligence was the major cause of the Irving Whale to sink.

The Irving Oil Company from the very beginning refused responsibility, also refusing to assume environmental damage or the cost of recuperating the 3100 tons of heavy "C" bunker oil and 7.2 tons of PCB's that went down with the Whale tanker.

The Canadian government pressured by environmental groups and the commercial fisherman had no choice, and took on the enormous challenge of trying to free the Irving Whale of its cargo. The project lasted from 1970 to 1996, it can be found on Internet under Environment Canada "History of the Irving Whale and the Recovery Project".

When considering **all costs** the Canadian Government possibly spent as much as a $100,000,000 to $200,000,000 million on the Irving Whale Project, all at Canadian taxpayers expenses.And to make matters worse, the Irving Whale was left to spill its oil and PCB's in the Gulf of St-Lawrence till 1996.It is extremely frustrating imagining that if the Irving Company collected on insurance for the Irving Whale saga (according to reports on internet) that they may have actually made money on this fiasco and left Canadian's paying the bill.

Mr. J. D. Irving is a major pillar of the Atlantic Salmon Federation, he is also a ringleader of the Clubs of the Restigouche River.Mr. J. D. Irving and the forestry practices of his logging company are promoted by the board of directors of the ASF as an excellent environmentalist a model for everyone (all logging companies) to follow if you are a subscriber to the writings of the ASF.

The Irving Whale's oil spill in the Gulf of St-Lawrence is one thing, but keeping from informing the government (according to CBC reports) that 7.2 tons of PCB's were on board until PCB's were detected in the oil spill during the clean up.

Spilling 7.2 tons of PCB's in the Gulf of St-Lawrence is the next worst thing to a nuclear disaster, this will leave the Gulf of St-Lawrence contaminated with one of the world's most toxic substance, contaminating our sea food for centuries to come.What in the world was the Canadian government thinking, letting the Irving Company walk away from this Horrendous Environmental Disaster scot-free?Or, maybe they were thinking.Thinking about the rewards and punishments that may accompany any decision to "rock the boat" or not to.

The Irving Whale issue must be brought back on the front burner, governments must be held accountable and the Irving Company must be assessed for the full costs of this disaster.

It is inconceivable that Atlantic salmon anglers, commercial cod fishermen and seal hunters remain so passive and accept whatever gets handed down to them by the billionaire pillars of the ASF leaving nothing for us to hand down to our future generations . . .

Literature is available on Internet: CBC "Irving Whale goes down" broadcast date: September 10, 1970 and CBC "Oil found on beaches of Magdalen Islands" broadcast date December 4, 1981, and much much more to be found on the subject.

****

The Quebec Salmon Federation

The Quebec Salmon Federation (FQSA) is a similar organization as the ASF, the main difference is in my opinion the FQSA's goal is oriented mostly toward economics and the wellbeing of its leaders, including special fishing privileges and rewards complimenting their position of power, conservation only comes following those priorities, Quebec salmon anglers get the leftovers.

For years the Government of Quebec Department of Fish and Game (M.L.C.P.) and the Department of Natural Resources were constantly at each other's throat. The Department of Fish and Game, then being its own Ministry, worked to protect fish and wildlife and their habitats, while the Department of Natural Resources was often destroying these for the exploitation of natural resources. This difference in position between these two departments got so intense that the Quebec Government handed over Fish and Game to the Department of Natural Resources. This move was done for one reason only, getting the Fish and Game Department out of the way, so D.N.R. could rape the forest without interruptions from the M.L.C.P., period!

With the Department of Natural Resources controlling both departments under the same Ministry the results are too predictable!

The Quebec Government handed over the keys to the hen-house to the fox.

Now that the Quebec Department of Natural Resources is in total control of the forest, with no interference from the Department of Fish and Game, the stage was set for massive abuses, and you can be sure there were some real dillies.

For decades I have told Mr. Côté of my deep concerns on what clear-cut-logging was doing to our salmon rivers and he was very well aware of what was happening.Once I realized that Mr. Côté, president of the FQSA, had no intention of stopping the massacre occurring in our forest and the devastating effect it was having on our salmon rivers I thought it was time that we both have a good talk.

In an intense discussion with Mr. Côté in Rimouski, I went straight to the point about clear-cut-logging, and he responded . . . "Pete you don't know what you're talking about, **beavers** do more damage to our salmon rivers then clear-cut-logging does".I knew exactly then without the slightest doubt which bed Mr. Côté was in and it certainly wasn't the Atlantic salmon conservation one. Following this conversation I scrutinized all of Mr. Côté's articles for over a decade, and never found a single word by him against logging.I guess this must mean that all the intense logging we have witnessed is actually good for the salmon rivers by taking food away from those evil beavers!I would not be surprised to see a "scientific" article about this being published in one of the federation journals.

During the late winter of 2005, I called Mr. Côté to let him know that I had managed to get all of Environment Canada's Data for the Restigouche River Basin and more.I made Mr. Côté aware of my findings at meter number 01BC001 just below the Kedgwick River where Mr. Côté operates a hunting and salmon fishing outfitting lodge.Also of the lower Restigouche and the Matapedia all with dramatic spring water yield increases of up to 450%, and peak low water flows up by an astounding 1592%.

(Graph of low water increase is available in chapter two)

Since Mr. Côté is president of the Quebec Salmon Federation it should have been **unquestionably a major issue** on his agenda. Nine months after our phone conversation and Mr. Côté receiving the documents in question, I met with Mr. Richard Firth the man in charge of the Restigouche River Basin for Quebec. I then asked Mr. Firth, if he had been made aware of my findings concerning water discharge at two meters on the Restigouche River.Mr. Firth answered, "what meters are you talking about Pete', 'Richard', I answered, 'the two meters on the Restigouche, meter numbers 01BC001 and meter 01BJ007'. He was dumbfounded, "Pete I did not even know there were water flow meters on the Restigouche River".

Mr. Côté president of the FQSA, after nine months following our conversation and receiving the data of water discharge for the Restigouche River Basin, had not even contacted Mr. Firth to inform him or said the slightest word about it. That is absolutely **incomprehensible** and **inexcusable!**

In the President's Chronicle "Saumons Ilimités" winter 2007.Mr. Yvon Côté once more is desperately trying to deflect the attention of anglers from the real issue, which is totally out of control clear-cut-logging in Quebec and New Brunswick.He states : "In spite of everything the salmon habitat in Quebec has been preserved against negative man-made influences."Mr. Côté has left out the extensive habitat destruction caused by countless dams constructed in the head waters of our salmon rivers for the log drives; he left out the frequent use of dynamite in our salmon rivers; he left out the countless use of bulldozers that have flatten many of our salmon rivers during log drives; he left out the dramatic increase of spring water yield of up to 450%, he left out the dramatic reduction in summer water flows; he left out the devastation caused by this dramatic increase in spring water yield provoking extremely massive ice in movement tearing the banks of the rivers to shreds; he left out that our salmon rivers are now one third wider than just fifty years ago; he left out that didymo was caused by a sewer dumping; he left out that there is no more trees left along the banks of our rivers and feeder creeks and now the sun has direct access to heat up our rivers;Mr. Côté also left out that logging is responsible for having created exactly what is required for the Didymo Algae to proliferate, a river that is shallow with slow moving warm water exposed to direct sunlight.

Mr. Yvon Côté wants the readers of his chronicle to believe that Quebec's environment was well protected, when reality shows totally the opposite.Quebec and New Brunswick have the world's worst forestry environmental record, even when compared to the United States.United States has over ten times more people density per square miles of land surface than Canada, but the USA has managed to save 25% of its land surface area as protected zones. Quebec on the other hand has only 4.8% of its land surface area as protected zones; to me this portends a complete total disaster for the future of Quebequers.

Environment truck getting ready to dump its sewage load in the Matapedia River

Above dump site is on the property of the Ministère des Transports of Quebec

Protection of the Environment Truck dumping its sewage load into the Matapedia River

Sewage entering the Matapedia River by pipe under railroad upstream from dumping site

Global Warming as of today has had at best caused a very small increase of our average summer water temperatures in the Northern Hemisphere, maybe a few degree, more or less.Over a long period of time this will become a much bigger problem and that is why we must address that problem as well.But that is not our most immediate problem!Imagine fishing on your favourite salmon river and the air temperature is a couple of degrees up or down, how much will that affect the water temperature?The fact is, very little, here is a comparison which explains what is making the difference in water temperature:Imagine having a stove in front of you with a large flat top and an even surface temperature throughout the entire stove top.Now with two pots containing exactly one gallon of water, both at room temperature.The only difference is that one of the pot has a diameter one third larger than the other pot,thus the larger diameter is shalower and has more surface tuching the heat of the stove.It is evident that the pot having the larger circonference with one third more surface tuching the heat of the stove and shallower water will reach the boilling point much MUCH faster than the narrower pot with less surface touching the heat and more water depth to bring to a boil.

The above comparison only includes the factor of a **wider** river, but not less water flow, remember one gallon in each pot.Lets compare it now with the **wider** pot having only a half a gallon of water in it, (the new summer water flows we are now experiencing) while the **narrower** pot is still holding one gallon of water (the narrower and deeper rivers we once had).The diagram in chapter two (Upsulquich River 1920 compared to 1991) demonstrates what a typical summer water flow used to be, and what it is today. Today our salmon rivers have only about half the volume of water flowing during the summer,and also add to the equasion the fact that the trees that once bordered our rivers are no longer there, allowing sunlight direct access to the surface of the water.During the low water period of the summer most of the water supply for the river comes from underground springs and small feeder brooks, which are usually very cold.A reduction in water supply means a much slower current, a slower current during the scorching heat of a summer will have its water surface exposed to the hot air and sun for a longer period from the time it enters the river, to when it leaves the estuary. More sunlight touching the slower moving water surface; the dark bottom of shallow bars; the dark rocks now petruding above water that captures heat from the sun and serve as heating elements, which will considerably increase water temperatures. The larger rocks and rock ledges can retain heat for hours after sunlight is off the river. It is not surprising at all as it is only common sence that water temperatures are today reaching the 80 + F on many of our salmon rivers due to distroyed habitat, **not global warming**! You can now understand why high water temperatures in our salmon rivers have very little to do with Global Warming.

I do not know everything about Mr Côté's affairs, but can clearly recognize without the slightest doubt that his first priority is definitely not Atlantic Salmon. To avoid any controversy about conflicts of interest Mr. Côté should publicly reveal the details of his present and past association with the logging industries he seems to be protecting so vigorously.

What puzzles me, how did Mr. Côté managed to acquire such an immense territory in the headwaters of the Kedgwick River, 196 square kilometres of woodland forest with exclusive hunting and fishing rights. Plus an extra portion of woodland territory surrounding the 196 square miles he owns, with some exclusive rights for a total of a 350 square kilometres of territory? This territory has one of the highest moose populations in the country, over 26 moose per ten square kilometres. Four annual moose hunting seasons, two bear limit, salmon and trout fishing, located on the main snowmobile and ATV trail. In other words an outfitter's paradise. Outfitters across Canada can **only dream** of owning such a huge territory with those kinds of exclusive rights.

At the present cost for woodland which is no less than $50,000.00 per hundred acres, a property like the one Mr. Côté owns should be evaluated at over $20,000.000.00 for the 196 square kilometres territory. Just the leasing value alone is worth several million dollars per year. The question is . . . how in the world did Mr. Côté manage to acquire such an immense territory, how did he manage to get such unbelievable privileges from the government. There is no question about it Mr. Côté managed things very well. The answer the public has a right to know are these: Who did Mr. Côté get these properties from? Was it from the logging industry? Was it the Quebec department of natural resources? How much did Mr. Côté pay for this valuable territory and rights or did he get it for free?

Mr. Côté's outfitting lodge is located on the Kedgwick River, smack in the middle of one of Eastern Canada's most affected areas from totally out of control clear-cut-logging. Is Mr. Côté blind or what, is it possible he cannot see the devastation right in his own backyard? What about the manager of his outfitting lodge Mr. Simon Lemay, a forest technician by profession, is it possible that his profession has not thought him to recognize when enough deforestation is enough?

People of Quebec are entitled to and must demand and GET answers form Mr. Côté . . .

Today the Didymosphenia geminata, a.k.a. "**Didymo**" or "rock snot" algae is in our salmon rivers. This algae was introduced in our salmon rivers by anglers with their equipment or boats contaminated from other rivers or lakes, **they tell us.** The fact is, for the Didymo algae to proliferate it needs warm, shallow, slow moving water and exposure to direct sunlight. In other words abusive clear-cut-logging is directly responsible for the Didymo proliferation in our salmon rivers. Please don't hold your breath waiting for the ASF or the F.Q.S.A. to admit it.It's business as usual for the ASF and the F.Q.S.A. seemingly protecting the logging industry while salmon anglers once more get the shaft.

The bottom line on **Didymo** indicates that it was caused by sewage dumpings along the Matapedia River.A dumping site was found in the back country on a steep side hill facing Fraser Brook; samples were taken at the site of the dumpings; at the mouth of Fraser Brook; in Alice Pool; behind the camp at Glenn Emma; and in the village of Matapedia.The samples were taken by Mr. Ted Flaherty, brother to the minister of finance for Canada, and Mr. Flaherty is an expert chemist in the field of pulp and paper. The five samples were sent to: The Pulp and Paper Research Institute on St-Jean Boulevard in Pointe-Claire, Quebec.

The results of above samples were sent to Mr. Richard Firth, general manager of the C.G.R.M.P. (the organization responsible for the Restigouche River Basin Quebec side) and I also received a copy from Mr. Flaherty for my records.

The report indicated that what everyone is calling the Didymo "rock snot, the paper like fibbers found on rocks in the Matapedia River", originated from sewage dumping's apparently from a paper-mill.According to the report "didymo" contained fibers of "unbleached aspen and birch wood product" identical to the ones being used in a paper- mill in Matane Quebec.

The intriging thing about this is that the C.G.R.M.P. never said one word about the report to anyone, and the F.Q.S.A.'s president Mr. Yvon Côté, is trying to cover-up these facts by writing an article that Didymo is caused by global warming and contaminants coming from New Zealand.

During the late nineties the Quebec Government authorized mega pig farms to be introduced in the headwaters of the Matapedia River.What in the world was the Quebec Government thinking of allowing mega pig farms in the headwaters of its best Salmon River? Well here is what I think was behind it all . . . If the Quebec government knew, and I'm sure they were well aware of the fact that the structure of the Matapedia River was rapidly deteriorating; and by introducing mega pig farms in the headwaters of the Matapedia knowing that later as problems like the Didymo; UDN; or furunculoses would invade the Matapedia River; the pig farms could be blamed and served as a scapegoat for the Government. The Department of Natural Resources who did not do its jobs of protecting the salmon habitat of the Matapedia from abusive logging and sewage dumping's would be off the hook, they'd have someone else to put the blame on and cover-up their mismanagement of the resource.This is just a theory but who knows!

The multinational companies like the Irving's, the Fraser's, the N.B.I.P., the Bowater's, the Bathurst papers Co., the Roland paper Co., to name a few have all played an important role in the destruction of our forest resources.Evidences clearly show that these companies first priority was to log as much and as quickly as it was possible, they were given open access to harvest our forest seemingly without the slightest regulations or surveillance.It was the Departments of Natural Resources **total and unconditional responsibility** to protect our forest and control logging practice.**<u>Why did D.N.R. not protect our forest or our rivers or our salmon?</u>**

Demanding a Royal Commission Inquiry

For the general public to be accurately informed as to what exactly has happened to our forests in Quebec and New Brunswick and who is responsible for the massacre. We should be all demanding an Independent Royal Commission Inquiry, with subpoena authority, to investigate all of the deputy ministers of the Department of Natural Resources from both provinces to hear their explanations and story.

Why the deputy ministers rather than the ministers? Because the deputy ministers are the ones who have evolved with the system; they are the ones who have all the contacts; they are the ones responsible for implementing the policies;they are the ones with the "hands on" experience;they are the ones responsible for the quotas and the forest inventory.There is no question that all the deputy ministers for the past five decades were all very well aware of what was happening in our forests, the question is, why did they not do anything to stop the massacre? Quebecquer's and New Brunswicker's have a right to know and should demand clear **honest** answers as to why the massacre of our forest was allowed and who is responsible?

Anyone involved in the destruction of the environment for profit, especially on this scale, and causing tens of thousands of people to lose their jobs and incalculable economic losses to working people and the government, should be considered criminals.Even further than that: government corruption, bribery, fraudulent reporting, endangering the public health, and tax evasion are crimes as well.I am reminded here of a quote from a judge in the old wild-west days:"You will be hanged after lunch, but first I need to give you a fair trial and find you guilty"

The city of Chandler, New Richmond and many other towns in the province of Quebec and New Brunswick who have suffered from the closures of its paper and saw mills, should be the first in demanding **honest** answers from the Departments of Natural Resources.The closure of each mill has a devastating effect throughout all of the population within that community.Most mills closed today were mostly due to gross negligence and or total incompetence from the Department of Natural Resources.How can the Quebec government explain spending over two hundred million dollars to renovate the mill in Chandler, and not reopen it? Hey people from Chandler wakeup, something is extremely wrong here.You should not have to suffer these consequences by yourselves.

Quebec can be proud of having the first **genuine conservation HERO** when it comes to preserving the forest in Canada. Mr. Richard Desjardins is Quebec's environment HERO, this man at the risk of his life, his career as a renowned singer, took on the logging industry and made a film on the devastation happening in Quebec's forest. The film is called "L`erreur Boréale" The Boreal Error. This film, a first of its kind in Canada, awakened Quebecquers in demanding a public inquiry on logging practices in the province.It resulted in the Coulomb inquiry, which clearly confirmed the devastation in Quebec's forest, recommending a very urgent reduction in forest removals.

Since Mr. Desjardins film was aired on Quebec television, the hardcore from the logging industry have been giving Mr. Desjardin a hard time, trying to discredit him and smearing his name in Quebec's media.And to make matters even worst the ring leader of these insult campaigns is a former Minister of Leisure Fish and Game and recently the Minister of Natural Resources. Mr. Guy Chevrette is now working for and defending the logging industry.Doesn't that say it all about how Mr. Chevrette operated when he was Minister of Natural Resources?

Mr. Pierre Corbeil now (as of 2007) is Minister of Natural Resources for the province of Quebec. During his mandate dozens of saw mills were closed in the province.While Quebec saw mills were being closed, thousands of truckloads of timber were travelling to other provinces or the US to be sawed.What in the world is Minister Corbeil thinking? Would you hire this guy to run your business?He has to be one of the most incompetent administrators in the government of Quebec. If that is the way for the Department of Natural Resources in Quebec to do business, no wonder the forests are in such a mess today.I have difficulty in believing that it is only the incompetence of the administrators from the Department of Natural Resources that is the cause of the problem.I suspect there is much more to this story than what appears on the surface.Again as stated earlier, it is what is going on under the surface that really matters.Answers could be provided through a Royal Commission Inquiry.

The purpose of this book was not written only to denounce the logging industry of its logging practices! But rather to inform the public, especially the loggers working in the woods, the paper-makers, sawmill operators, and anglers whom are all the victims of these abuses made by a handful of multinational companies who can be trusted only to look out for themselves.I am repeating myself once more but I just hope that everyone affected by these abuses recognizes that they have legal and moral rights.Both Departments of Natural Resources from Quebec as well as from New Brunswick have a lot of explaining to do and let's not forget to question the other organizations, federations, and foundations that have been subverted to the dark side by the logging interests.

When one read David Suzuki's letter addressed to me, (**in chapter five**) saying "We have done stories on clear-cut logging before and have been hammered by the forest industry. Right now the CBC is under siege and **terrified** in getting into more controversy".When you have river administrators like Richard Firth who have said in a reunion "if I interfere trying to stop Clear-cut-logging they will kill me, and I don't mean killing me as an expression I mean six feet underground".Most river administrators are aware of what clear-cut-logging is doing to their rivers, but are terrified of speaking about it.A guy like Richard Firth does not have much choice but to go with the flow, if he rocks the boat he will lose his job.Every river administrator I have had private conversation with have told me the same thing.Guys like Mr. Yvon Côté president of the Quebec Salmon Federation should be a leader in confronting the forest industry.The same goes for the ASF.But not one single word from these guys and they surely seem to be drawing valuable privileges as a reward for their silence.

MAGIC IN THE AIR . . .

It's too beautiful to let it be destroyed . . .

Chapter Four

A BRIGHT FUTURE and PROSPERETY

.

Many of us have read these words in the pages of the Atlantic Salmon Federation Journal so many times in the past that they have become almost cliché; **"A Bright Future for Atlantic Salmon"** and we have all seen the actual results of the ASF's . . . Bright Future!

The ASF reminds me of the following scenario: A chicken farmer who has free ranging chickens around his farm, and within the immediate area there is an over population of foxes, one day the chicken farmer is scratching his head in disbelief, wondering . . . **Where the hell are all my chickens going?**Meanwhile, The Farmer's Chicken Federation is desperately trying to brainwash its members that they have performed countless studies on fox stomach content and have never found the slightest chicken particle whatsoever in fox stomachs.In this ridiculous scenario all of us can quickly understand why the farmer is losing his chickens.This is an admittedly simple minded example, but the flip side of this analogy is much more complex.The Atlantic salmon is a migratory creature travelling thousands of miles across rivers; bays; gulfs; straits; and oceans, involving a variety of uncertain and unverifiable situations. Obviously one can recognize that due to the immense travelling territory of Atlantic salmon migrations, how easy it is for regulatory agencies corrupted by big money and politics and scientists whose research is bought and paid for by self serving corporate and private interests to misinform the public about the reality of what is happening here in the North Atlantic. People responsible for monitoring and reporting and regulating the valuable natural resources in our oceans and rivers can devise all sorts of reasons to cover-up any situation and/or report any findings they wish to concoct. It is almost impossible to pin down a fraud when it is perpetrated by a clever scientist or a government official with bent political objectives. Convenient excuses abound; climate change, global warming, water temperatures, ocean currents, diseases, ice movements, food shortage, pollution, just to name a few.One thing we know for sure, our fishery is in deep trouble in the North Atlantic. Government policy to date has resulted in a permanent state of misery for the working class.Extraordinary measures are needed now.A royal commission inquiry is totally necessary at this time in order to expose corruption and establish a new road map to the full recovery of a fishery industry and the lives of thousands of Maritime workers, that has been all but destroyed by terrible government policies based on power politics and false science.

The dramatic decline of our fisheries in the North Atlantic is of major concern to many of us who depend on the resource for our livelihood.Just the fact of recognizing the degraded state the North Atlantic Fisheries is an extremely frustrating and a heartbreaking situation. The enormity of this problem is almost overwhelming but we cannot remain passive to such a horrible situation; it is our future and those of our children and future generations.The purpose of this book is to sound an alarm.I am not the first to do so but all the warnings that have been sounded to date have not affected the changes that are needed.It is my desire to ring a very loud bell in the ears of the people of the North Atlantic coast and to cause them to question the decisions of the powers that be and to expose the secret powers who are hiding behind the powers that be.The reason I am able to do this is because I was lucky enough to be born into a

family who, for 3 generations, have managed the largest Atlantic Salmon Fly Fishing outfitters in the world.It is very important that people understand the culture of this environment.Over the centuries, fishing for Atlantic Salmon has evolved into an elite art originating on the private fishing waters of the vast estates of European nobility.It has often been referred to as the "sport of kings" and this is not a joke.Atlantic Salmon fishing is the most prestigious, exciting, and exclusive fishing experience on the planet and this experience, until relatively recently, has been reserved only for the private enjoyment of the wealthy upper class.

All others who dare to intrude on these private waters are "poachers" and even up to the present day the crime of poaching carries severe penalties.The modern phenomenon of Atlantic Salmon fishing is focused on Atlantic Canada where the greatest Salmon Rivers in the world converge.To our location at the confluence of the Restigouche and Matapedia River have journeyed the rich and the powerful and the famous.US Presidents from Grover Cleveland to Eisenhower to moguls of big business, old money and nouveau riche alike, many of the greatest actors and athletes of our age, foreign dignitaries too numerous to mention, and last, but certainly not least, a host of our Canadian government officials seeking to enjoy the privileges of their rank and power and the opportunity to rub shoulders with persons of wealth and celebrity.There is something about a Salmon river that acts as a great equalizer, albeit temporarily, which allows these great and powerful individuals to bond closely with their guides and to frequently relieve the stress of the outside world by casual conversation often confiding personal matters and issues with the guide.It has been my privilege for the past 48 years to live and work in this fantastic environment at the heart and center of the Atlantic Salmon business and the information that I have learned from these people, many of whom are individuals of extraordinary intelligence and ability, is information that news reporters would die for.In fact this would nearly cost me my own life as will be discussed later.This is not just a kiss and tell book where secret conversations of a bunch of big shots are revealed exposing the institutional corruption in certain Public Interest Federations and New Brunswick Provincial Government.I have earned my place at the table having also devoted a lifetime to study, research, observe, listen and to obtain all the knowledge that I can possibly learn about all things related to The Atlantic Salmon.It is vital that I pass this information on to anglers, commercial fishermen, Aboriginal Peoples, and the general public, so that others, especially those who will follow in the future, will be able to build on this foundation of facts, correcting my errors which may be many, and most importantly understand how totally connected this fabulous fish is with the entire ecosystem of the North Atlantic and Maritime Canada.General Douglas MacArthur once made a now famous quote: " a chain is only as strong as its weakest link".In the "chain" of ecological balance and biodiversity, the Atlantic Salmon, the so called king of all fish, has proven to be the "weak link" as we observe the situation in Eastern Canada.This brings the big picture into clear focus by exposing the man made environmental disasters and horrendous environmental crimes which have affected not only the Atlantic Salmon as a wild species, but also the lives of ordinary people so severely and continue to threaten our future well being. After understanding the issues causing the North Atlantic fisheries collapse we will all want to become agents of change.Outrage and anger will be the natural reaction of many people but after much anguish over this issue, I now see that anger by itself will not solve the problems and I firmly believe that the future does not need to be so bleak and negative.Cleaning up the mess and reforming the policies born of corruption is a task for the present generation.We cannot avoid this responsibility, there will be a hard fight, but there is no question that ordinary people will decide these matters.In a decade of time significant improvements can be made

and the benefits of reform can be clearly demonstrated.Refinements of the reformed policies will be ongoing based on honest science, proven results, and fairness to ordinary people.Strict adherence to clean water measures must be maintained by future generations as a life or death matter.Public education on this issue must be mandatory. It is essential that no pollution of any kind be introduced into our rivers by towns or villages or farms or industry.In theory this is the law today, but it is a bad joke and everyone with eyes and a brain knows this to be true. Too many people including government regulatory officials are getting away with environmental murder.Enough people getting angry will change this situation quickly.

What can be done?

I believe the root of the problem is in our federations, in conspiracy with the corporate titans of the logging industry and the billionaire riparian owners mainly from the Restigouche River. These individuals need to be removed from positions of control of our federations; the public has to take over what is rightly theirs in the first place.

Here is an expression that I find appropriate for this situation in the vocabulary of the legendary Richard Nelson Adams:

'' We've got to get the Rats out of the barn! ``

That describes clearly what I think needs to be done.

Salmon anglers must take control of their salmon federations, it is unacceptable that the Atlantic Salmon Federation not hold its annual meetings where all members can participate in the voting process. The present monopoly "Clubs of the Restigouche River" of the ASF must be stopped, the ASF must be accessible by all of its members and not just for a select group. Its headquarters should be relocated in a region near a Salmon River where the bulk of its members are located.Its annual general assembly must be held near a salmon oriented town, in a large hall accessible to all of its members with an open verifiable voting system. And **please** no annual dinner's like it is presently at $500.00 a plate, it must be affordable for all members.

Seal Overpopulation is the Cause of our Fisheries Decline.

As politically sensitive as it may be our Federations and Governments have to start informing the world about the potential **chaos** anticipated if seal and common whale population explosion is not brought under control.

Television documentaries, scientific publications, books on the subject of seal and whale hunting must be available to accurately inform the world of what is at stake if seal hunting is stopped.

In Raoul Jomphe's documentary film aired during March of 2007, Mr. Jomphe demonstrated how the activists managed to film the spectacular seal-hunting scene that shocked the world. Showing seal pups being skinned while apparently still alive in front of the cameras, it is now known that these scenes were all orchestrated by these activists where the seal hunters were paid to put on these shows for them to film.

It is evident that ignorance is at the root of the seal hunt conflict, donors who finance activists to put on a show to stop the seal hunt, are not accurately and properly informed of the consequences of their demands. A complete seal hunt ban would totally ruin Canada's Atlantic Coast fishery and it would be devastating to seal also, Atlantic cod, and Atlantic salmon stocks would collapse, they would be totally decimated by a seal hunt ban. Thousands upon thousands of jobs have already been lost from the partial seal hunt ban since 1974. These activists don't realise that seal population can affect not only the immediate Atlantic Coast, it affects all of our salmon rivers, from Labrador to Maine and from Newfoundland to Quebec. These areas once had large runs of Atlantic salmon and an immense cod population, today Maine's Atlantic salmon is on the endangered list and so as many salmon rivers on the East Coast. Putting the situation in perspective it is certainly inconceivable to stop seal hunting knowing in advance if completely stopped seal would eventually die of starvation, creating an ecological tragedy and an economic disaster for Eastern Canada and the U.S.What the **donors** of anti seal hunting activists believe they are going to obtain by a total seal-hunting ban, is totally the opposite result they will be accomplishing.

Let's imagine as an example that a total ban on deer hunting is implemented in the United State, the outcome of such a ban can be easily predicted in advance.Within five years following the ban there would be deer everywhere, millions of road kills annually; deer eating people's garden; flowers around people's house; it would feel; it would look; it would sound; and it would smell just like a rat or a cockroach infestation. Eventually diseases would spread throughout the deer heard and so as other animals in contact including people's pets.With the ending result, deer dying by the hundreds of thousands from diseases and starvation.It is just simple common sense; deer so as seals and whales need to be properly managed for animals to acquire optimal health and a lower stressed environment.

I was listening to a lady activist comments on CBC National News on March 15, 2007.She said, "we will pay all the seal hunters to stay home" it is clear this lady doesn't have the slightest clue of what she is talking about. Since the seal hunt was stopped in 1974, it is tens of billions $$$ annually the North Atlantic Coast has lost, thousands upon thousands of jobs and she's thinking that by just paying a few seal hunters from Madeleine Island to stay home that this would be a fair compensation.

(Donations to animal activist groups **skyrockets** when a seal hunt debate is on.)Millions of dollars are donated per month to these seal activist organisations . . . It is worth hundreds of millions of dollars "**big bucks**" to have a seal **hunt** conflict for the administrators of these organisations.

The conclusion . . .

The losers: The big losers of the seal hunting saga are first, the seals themselves, now having to struggle to compete for sufficient food to survive, they are now on the edge of starving to death. Secondly, the thousands of commercial cod fishermen, seal hunters and salmon anglers on the North Atlantic Coast whom have lost their jobs and livelihood due to the seal hunting conflict. And thirdly, the totally misinformed donors of these activist groups who have been mislead and told only the side of the story that would get them to cough-up the most donations.Hey! . . Who would not get in a white outfit looking like a seal impregnated with blood, (red dye) and roll over for a couple of days in the streets of Washington D.C. every year with a few buddies in front of the media, if it could generate for the boys over $50,000,000.00 a year?I can tell you, I'd put on some hell of a show for that kind of money!

The winners: By far the clear winners of the seal hunt saga are without the slightest doubt the activist groups, who are living a lavish lifestyle from the hundreds of millions in donations, also the riparian owners (Salmon Fishing Clubs) and the logging industry. Following a seal hunt conflict seal activists have a bank account bursting with hundreds of millions in donations, ready to delightfully travel the world first class at the seal donor's expenses.Imagine, the president of the Humane Right Society for the Protection of Animals pays himself a wage of more than four times the annual salary of the Prime Minister of Canada, plus a lavish lifestyle travelling around the world all expenses paid at the seal donor's expenses. Seal hunt conflicts have become a media travesty of unprecedented proportions, catching the attention of millions of listeners around the world whom are suck-into what is nothing but a sham by misleading information. I'm convinced that once the activist groups get closer to their pretended goal of completely stopping the seal hunt**, they'll back off!** If the seal hunt is completely stopped, they'll lose hundreds of millions in future donations and I'm sure they don't want that to happen at all.

It is the responsibility of our Canadian governments to educate the public about seal and whale hunting, and the consequences of a seal-hunting ban.

We must start by **properly informing and educating** the world on the impact seals and whales are having on our fish stocks, people's lives and the chaos if a balanced food chain is not acquired. The world must understand that Canada so as the U.S. have the moral obligation and duty to manage its wildlife resources to the best of its ability for future generations.If Canada and the U.S. keep on doing nothing just to save their image is in my opinion unacceptable. If Canada's and the U.S. East Coast fisheries is not brought back generating jobs as in the past and having a real economic impact for the region, then the incentive for protecting it will fade away.

Why in the world is the government of Canada and the U.S. not filing lawsuits for billions of dollars in damage against the Human Right Society for the Protection of Animal, Green Peace and the Sea Shepherds? These activists have been spreading misleading propaganda campaigns against Canadian seal hunters for years. They are advertising that Canadian seal hunters are still killing white seal pups, when they know very well that the harvesting of white seal pups was banned for over twenty years. Why is the Canadian government just sitting there and accepting these abuses by these activist groups?I believe there are sufficient evidences to conclude that the logging industry and the riparian owners are at the root of this seal hunt conflict and controlling the government agenda so nothing gets done.

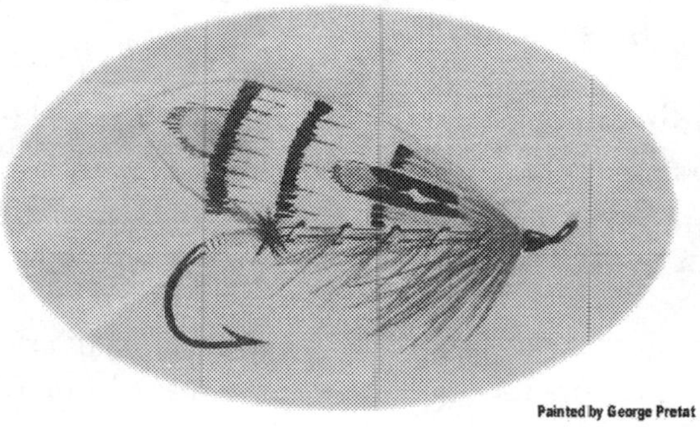

Painted by George Pretat

Canada's Atlantic Coast . . . Enormous Potential.

In this modern day and age where most markets are saturated with marginal potential for development, unless, substantial investments are made to generate capital returns.

Imagine a project that would not require one single penny of investment by our governments and generate ten's of billions of dollars annually . . . Is this possible?It certainly is!

The only criteria required from our governments to acquire this manna are, implement applicable rules, laws with teeth and very strict controls, believe it or not that is all that is required to jumpstart a multibillion dollar industry.

One has just to pay a little attention when shopping in any of North America's grocery-stores you'll observe shelves and refrigerators loaded with salmon from Alaska and Western Canada, why can't Eastern Canada have the same fisheries for its residents?Obviously something has definitely gone wrong, we need to know more and get answers from our governments . . .

The project:

The Canadian government must be prepared to introduce appropriate legislation prior to going forward with a mega seal and whale hunt project. **Extremely severe penalties** to anyone interfering with the hunts; penalties in the tens of thousands of dollars per day per individual who would break the law; the seizure of all equipment used including their boat, ship, helicopter or whatever was used to interference with the hunt; plus a mandatory jail sentence.We can no longer permit the travesty of the magnitudes experienced during the past three decades.Our governments have to show leadership, step to the plate and not be intimidated by a few billionaires like J. D. Irving or environmentalists groups trying to derail this project.

The Atlantic Coast has enormous potential, I am very optimistic that in the near future once our federations are no longer under the control of the riparian owners and the logging industry. Anglers, commercial fishermen, seal hunters and governments should all join in and get this "**bold new project**" for the Atlantic Coast jumpstarted.

Considerations:

Considering that the seal population in the North Atlantic could be now surpassing the 20,000,000 strong growing to alarming levels and seals starving to dead.

Considering that some of our common whale populations (whale of 1000 to 10,000 lbs.) could be now surpassing the 6,000,000 strong in the North Atlantic.

Considering that there has been no controls of seal and whale population, which has exploded in the last three decades, now putting enormous strain on the North Atlantic food chain. The food chain in the North Atlantic is today totally out of whack, with a dramatic decrease of herring, salmon and cod stock's as a result due to the lack of predator control.

Considering that presently there are no programs or orientations offering realistic meaningful measures to accomplish concrete results for improving our fish stocks on the North Atlantic Coast.

Considering that the present status quo is unacceptable, extremely costly preventing tens of thousands of jobs and billions in revenues for the North Atlantic Coast, also that chaos is just around the corner if the status quo remains.

Considering that other countries have shown that bold project to control the balance of nature can work. On Galapagos Islands over twenty thousand wild goats were slaughtered to gain control of the echo balance on these islands, and done so without the interference of other countries and delivered outstanding results.

Considering that Canada has not really tried to inform or educate the environmental donors of the serious consequences of doing nothing with the seal and whale population.

I believe that Atlantic Canada and the Northern U.S. states are now ready to accept and fight for a **bold new project** to control seal and whale populations, considering the immense economical advantage in the billions of dollars per year for the entire region.

D.F.O.'s scientists have recently reported . . . "seal population has now stabilized due to birth rate which has gone down by as much as 70%", in other words, D.F.O.'s scientists are telling us that seals are starving to death due to overpopulation.

What Atlantic Canada needs is to improve its fishery and create enormous wealth for the region with a bold seal and whale hunt program.

Economics:

Thousands upon thousands of jobs will be created by a well scientifically based major seal and whale hunt program, with modern technology and innovation for transforming the biomass in dozens of new products. Modern plants along the Atlantic Coast would open up creating thousands of new jobs by producing from: collagen; the best of Bio grade A meat; soap; dog food; cat food; cattle feed; omega 3 oil; fertiliser; leather goods; multiple fur and leather clothing; etc. etc. Then our Salmon Rivers would fill up again plumb full of salmon, commercial cod fishermen could resume their cod fishery within a decade and the list is endless with potential. And the most amazing fact of all our governments would not even be asked to invest one single penny, it only requires appropriate laws and regulations to be implemented so the private investors would feel protected.

Let's take a close look at what a MEGA seal and whale hunt program could generate for the Atlantic Coast:

Let's assume that the initial objective is to annually harvest 30% of specifically selected seal heard and 5% of common whale population inside Canada and Maine's Atlantic Coast 200 miles limit to stabilize the food chain.

Let's assume that the selected seal population within these boundaries is in the excess of ten million, and that the small fish eating whale is exceeding three million.

According to knowledgeable people in the field it is said that a matured seal can generate up to $1,500.00 when all parts are used to its full potential, and whale biomass can generate over $5.00 a pound.

A quick calculation: Harvesting 3 million seals and 150,000 whales could generate up to $7,500,000,000.00 annually. Creating possibly over 20,000 jobs for the harvesting, the processing and the manufacturing of goods.

Following a decade of seal and whale population control, cod stocks should have grown to a point where reopening commercial cod fishing should be possible, creating thousands of new jobs, increasing the economic downfall on the East Coast in the billions annually. New investment by commercial fishermen for fishing boats, including equipment of all sorts, openings of existing factories or the building of new ones, innovating in new processing plans for second and third transformations of biomass.

To put things in perspective, if the Salmon River in Pulaski upstate New York can generate with just seventeen miles of river an economic downfall of over $25,000,000.00 annually, imagine what our rivers could do if it was properly administered for the wealth of the population?

Imagine if our WORLD Atlantic salmon population estimated at 2,000,000 today could grow to hundreds of millions for the entire North Atlantic, it could generate billions annually to the sport fishery. Compounding all of these new resources together including the cod fishery, the seal and whale hunt program you would have created a mega economy.

The Miracle of Wild Atlantic Cod, Wild Atlantic Salmon, Seal and Whale Produce:

Health Benefits of Omega 3 Fatty Acids on Our Population:

Did you know that countless scientific studies have clearly demonstrated that the major cause of most North American diseases originate from the chronic shortage of Omega 3 Fatty Acid's in North American diet. North American's have been fed during the last four decades a diet way too rich in Omega 6 Fatty Acids.A high diet in Omega 6 Fatty Acid is directly responsible for countless cancers, heart diseases, arthritis, chronic inflammation and depression.

North American's have been feeding its livestock for the past three to four decades with a high corn and meat diet rich in Omega 6 Fatty Acids. Instead if it switched feed for its livestock to seal and whale meat, it could dramatically increase the Omega 3 Fatty Acids content of our table meat.

A diet rich in Omega 3 Fatty Acids in meat and a readily large supply of fresh Atlantic Wild Cod and Wild Atlantic Salmon could dramatically reduce Medicare cost by billions of dollars for Canadians annually.Depression could be reduced dramatically just by having Canadians increasing their intake of high quality Omega 3 Fatty Acids from Wild Atlantic Cod, Wild Atlantic Salmon, Seal and Whale produce.The annual cost of antidepressant prescriptions for Canadian is astounding, in the billions of dollars, so as absentees form work and reduced productivity due to poor concentration.Canadian pet owners could benefit dearly from food mix manufactured with the leftover of seal and whale meat, our pets have suffered the same severe Omega 3 Fatty Acid depletion as we humans.Extensive vet cost could be dramatically reduced and our pets would be much healthier.

A decade following a well managed North Atlantic Fisheries, our rivers would be plumb full of Atlantic salmon, there would be no need for catch and release, thus allowing anglers to harvest their catch and consuming more of the super healthy essential fatty acids.

Come on Atlantic Canada and the U.S., rise to the occasion . . . It's **your** pot of gold at the end of the rainbow and it's just within reach.

Predator controls:

Controlling all of the predators is a must, the great number of mergansers, cormorants and kingfishers need to be also brought under control for the North Atlantic to achieve its full potential.

What our rivers will need:

Start immediate and gradual removal of all foreign material deposited by four decades of erosion due to mismanagement of our forestry programs.

The re-stabilization of all our river banks with large rocks.

Encouragement of vegetation growth and the replacement of trees along the river banks.

No more cutting within two hundred meters of any river including feeder brooks.

The longer we wait the more it will cost to solve the problems and the less probable it will be to accomplish these ends.

The effect of years of massive clear-cutting will be with us for a century, to neutralise some of its negative impact on our rivers, an icebreaker should be used every spring to break-up the ice in the mid and lower parts of the Restigouche.

The WABANAKY (Ice Breaker) on the Restigouche River

When the Restigouche dumps its ice, it is crucial that this ice keeps flowing continually, and that it does not jam and come to a stop.Every ice pile-up that occurs on the Restigouche, provokes extensive damage to the structure of the river, literally ripping it apart.Perhaps the logging industry should be forced to share the cost of this annual service.

Quebec's original plan for the Wabanaky was to break up the ice in the New Brunswick channels only, leaving the Quebec channels with ice intact behind the islands.The plan had to be altered due to intervention form the Department of Natural Resources of New Brunswick, who restrained the Wabanaky from breaking most ice in the Restigouche River New Brunswick channels.The decision to ward off the Wabanaky from the New Brunswick side of the Restigouche River was one of ignorance; a bad decision taken by people who do not understand the mechanics and the function of the work done by the icebreaker.

Canoeists travelling in the lower end of the Restigouche River on the Quebec side where ice breaking work was done, quickly recognized the favourable improvements of channel depth, and the dramatic increase in water flow to the detriment of New Brunswick channels were the icebreaker did not break the ice. While on the New Brunswick side, we observed a noticeable deterioration of the channels, pools and water flow.Thus, if original recommendations of ice breaking had continued as planned, the channels in the lower end of the river New Brunswick side of the Restigouche would have dramatically improved.It is not too late for the New Brunswick Department of Natural Resources to change its stand . . .

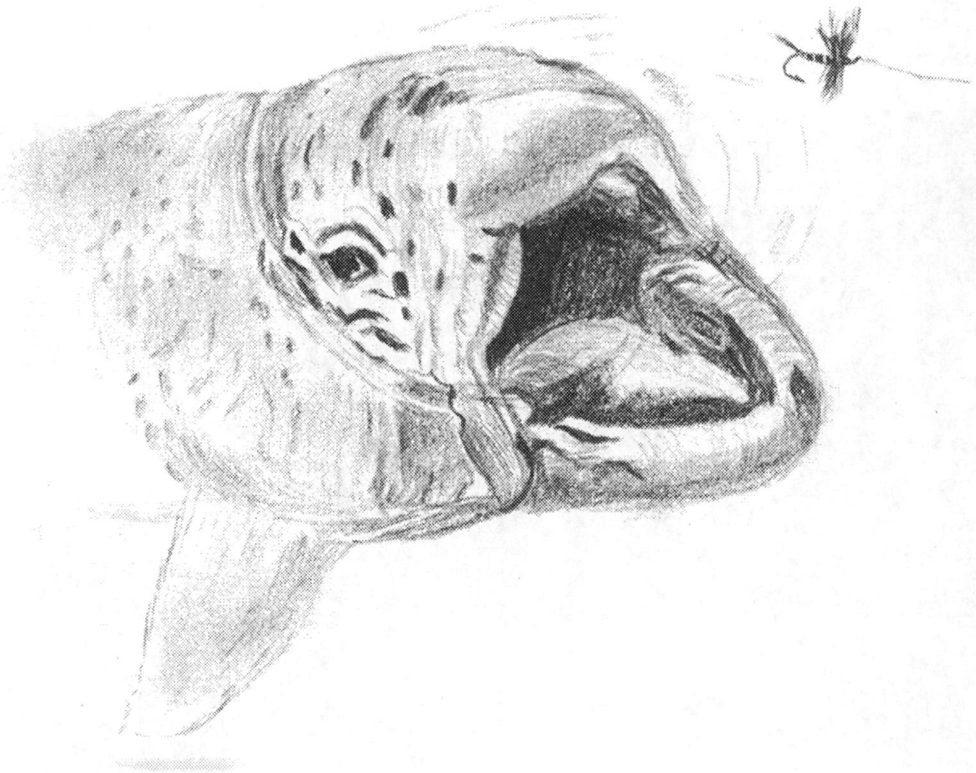

Chapter Five

Summary and Conclusion

Summary and conclusion:

Water, food and pollution are issues of extreme concern for the world population, however during the next half century these concerns will become critical factors to the survival of civilization as we know it.Costly and innovative methods will need to be implemented for the modernization of our way of life.There can be no questions or arguments about continuing the status quo.Urgent change is vital.This means that all production of future energy and food and goods and services will need to be carried out with the most non-polluting technologies available, especially for our food supply.The USA will double its population in the next half a century. The water supply is already a major concern for much of the USA.Much of our arable land has been depleted of its topsoil by erosion and contaminated by pesticides and chemicals of all sorts.The wind itself carries poisonous industrial pollutants half way across the continent where these toxic substances are deposited with disastrous consequences.We have known about these issues for decades.More recently we have become aware of the so called "greenhouse gasses" and their effect on climate change.Why can't we seem to get on top of these issues and make better progress implementing solutions rather than endlessly debating what is obvious to all?

The answers to these problems is extremely complex, however the answer to why we have not made better progress is easy.Up to now our governments have operated and made decisions only with the concern of the political outcomes of these policies. In other words the only criteria for our political leaders and lawmakers is how many votes and $$$ for the party will be generated for the next election.Critical issues affecting our very survival and the critical solutions which are the key to our future prosperity, have become nothing more than public relations and marketing tools used by big corporations and their political operatives who set the agenda and thus control government. In short we can no longer operate under these political restrictions.Governments have to regulate with intelligence and with incentives rewarding innovative technologies which ensure the best outcomes for society and the generations to come. Anything less should be considered disgracefully incompetent.Some of the more serious shortcomings in this arena are actually the result of dishonesty and political corruption, which at this level and with so much at stake, could even be considered as treason.

Animal rights groups and environmental activists are the recipients of extraordinary government largess as well as grants, gifts and donations from wealthy individuals and corporations.They have become big industries unto themselves and they have big budgets and they are professionals at influencing and intimidating political decision makers. They are also quite at home in the courtroom and have frequently established a strangle hold on government policy decisions, often forcing policies to be adopted that are only for their group's special interests.These groups have gained tremendous economic and political power over the past half a century along with the political parties that accommodated them. I have talked intensively about these activist groups in earlier chapters and would like to point out again that all of these organisations have one mission and one goal in common which is to generate money for their piggy-bank.This is especially true for the very lucrative seal and whale campaigns.Some of these activist groups could do the world a much greater favour by concentrating their efforts by stopping big industries from polluting our waterways and oceans, but there's no money to be made with a boring subject like environment. They have to have sensationalised subject, like white seal pups being hit over the head with a club on blood spattered snow. What unbelievable material (footage) this makes for a propaganda campaign that generated tens, if not hundreds of millions of dollars in donations since the start of the fabricated media travesties regarding those dreadfully abused white seal pups.

Whales and seals compete with humans in the great cycle of inter-dependent relationships we call the food chain, just like all other animals on the planet are competing with one another for their survival. Everyone, including vegetarians and animal lovers, needs to face this reality at some point. It is a rough and tough world out there and life for many species consists of becoming food for another.Human beings have long ago learned to manage many of the land and water species we consume. We have also to improve our techniques over many millenniums since the beginning of civilization; however we urgently need to get even better at this management especially for those species that live in the oceans.

There are seventy-five to eighty different types of whales around the globe.One of the smallest ones, the Minke Whale is estimated to consume 10 kilograms of fish per kilogram of body mass, which puts a heavy predatory pressure on commercial species of fish.Some reports have shown that cetaceans (whales) and pinnipeds (sea lions and seals) are estimated to eat 600 million tons of fish per year, compared to with just 150 million tons by humans.

When accounting for the huge fossil fuel energy required to produce the world's food supply through farming, and the massive land deforestation required for farming, (deforestation is responsible for 25% of greenhouse gas effect in Canada) and the impact of farming on our rivers and lakes from the pollution run-off from farming. One can easily recognize the unlimited advantages to be gained from utilizing a non-polluting ocean food supply. Of course modern land farming techniques will continue to provide substantial nutrition to much of the world; however our oceans have to become the world's major supply of healthy food in the future. The great oceans which cover three quarters of the earth's surface have the proven potential to generate a wide variety of healthy food products, hundreds of millions of tons per year, but we must stop polluting these oceans. Properly managed our oceans can, in turn, give the world in return an incredibly abundant food supply and leaving behind only negligible impact on the environment.

Proper ocean management means managing the populations of inter-related species.I do not know of anyone that would not want to see the world of animal kingdom different, with all species respecting each other, no big fish eating smaller fish, no lion penetrating its claws deep in the flesh of a gazelle desperately trying to outrun its predator.Many good and intelligent people have lived their lives in cities and see only a world of concrete and plastic and images on TV.Many of them have only had brief exposure to the outdoors; many of them have never had, and have no interest in, experiencing outdoors activities such as hunting or fishing.Many of them even oppose such activities as being inhumane or barbaric. They have no frame of reference for the real world of nature. In some abstract way they realize that it is a tough world out there in the wilderness, and they are uncomfortable in this environment. These are the people who get sucked into anti-hunting movement, and the animal rights movement.The kind heartedness of these people has been captivated by the misinformation and propaganda of activist groups who flood their mail boxes and TV screens with false promises that generous donations will further a cause and help reform the world of the nature into something more kind and gentle.

This travesty can only be reversed by education.The more people become accurately informed the more it will become possible for our governments to do what really needs to be done with regards to managing our oceans for the best of all concerned.Scientifically and humanely managed oceans are the key to the future food supply for the world increasing populations. World governments can no longer accept the present status-quo, we need to **severely** sanction ocean polluters and start on a new path for developing scientific and humane methods of controlling the giant herds of seals, humble squid and other predators roaming the oceans and ravaging our valuable and irreplaceable fish stocks so that these resources can sustain us for thousands of years to come.

Technologies are out there to dramatically reduce pollutants in our environment.As an example **hemp** uses no dioxin bleach to make paper and it can be whitened with hydrogen peroxide which doesn't poison our waterways as chloride and bleach does. The USDA reported as early as 1916 that an acre of hemp produced as much paper as four acres of trees annually.

Three of the United States founding fathers cultivated hemp, the United States Constitution, so as the Declaration of Independence is written on hemp paper. Hemp produces very high quality paper, it can keep forever, never turning yellow like paper from trees. Major General George Washington, first president of the United States cultivated hemp as a crop on his farm. Thomas Jefferson, the principal author of the American Declaration of Independence, which he drafted on hemp paper, was the third president of the United States. He cultivated hemp as a crop.Benjamin Franklin, started the first American paper mill, which made paper exclusively from hemp.

Pollution was important to Rudolf Diesel and he saw in his engine a solution to the inefficient, highly polluting engines of his time, (diesel engines pollute 40% less than gas engines) but the DuPont, Mellon, and Hearst interests soon put a stop to Diesel's plans. **http://www.hempcar.org/diesel.shtml**Hemp is the best option for producing Bio-Diesel Fuel to run automobiles. According to scientific reports, hemp is at the top of the list for the most efficient substance for producing Bio-Diesel fuel to run diesel engines and considerably reduces air pollution. I recommend the readers to search the Internet for Dioxin and Hemp; you'll be amazed at what you'll learn about how big corporations have promoted government programs and legislation which benefit these companies financial interest at the expense of the public interest.

Look up: http://www.jackherer.com/chapters.html make sure to read Jack's chapter nine, also search the Internet to read all about hemp, you'll be chocked at what you'll learn . . .

It is truly amazing when one recognizes the astounding similarities in the facts surrounding the conspiracies involving Governments and Big Corporate Interests as they worked together to cover-up the unprecedented destruction of the environment and destroy the Agricultural Hemp Industry and the Atlantic Salmon Industry.Exactly the same tactics were involved as both conspiracies utilized their corporate media as a platform to manipulate the facts and create a bogus scenarios and false conclusions.Both conspiracies used pseudo-science and also purchased specific results from scientific studies to brainwash the public with misleading, and frequently totally false, propaganda.

Unbiased scientific information about the agricultural properties and benefits of Hemp are widely available today.This conspiracy has been exposed widely and written about by others.

http://www.sdearthtimes.com/et0199/et0199s11.html

http://democratequalssocialist.wordpress.com/2007/11/30/dioxin-dow-dupont-hemp/

No bigger pack of lies or packaging of massive "scientific baloney" has ever been mounted in the history of North America than what has been done in the incredible scandal campaign by Big Corporate Interests and Government against the agricultural Hemp industry.The more one is informed about Hemp, the more one gets outraged at governments for allowing mainly the chemicals, paper and oil companies to perpetrate false science, manipulate the facts and thereby set the stage for the passage of ridiculously self-serving and unnecessary laws and allowing the needless destruction of our environment.Easily, more than half of the trees that have been cut in the last century would still be alive and growing if the agricultural Hemp industry had been permitted to reach its full potential.North America would not have ended up with such badly slaughtered forest, its rivers and streams largely destroyed, its fish stocks poisoned, and its air as badly polluted. Not to even mention the extraordinary impact of this Corporate-Government blundering on the global warming issue.

These same companies especially Monsanto, DuPont and Dow, all profited immensely with trillions of dollars of revenues between them during the pass half a century are still at it again today with the full blessing from our corrupted governments.Just take corn farming as a example, corn has doubled in price between 2007 and 2008, (according to a CBC report in November of 2008) and wouldn't you know it, prices for fertiliser, pesticides, and herbicides for corn cultivation has also doubled during the same period.How can governments have encouraged corn crops for ethanol production, it is known that in cultivating enough corn to produce a 100 gallons of ethanol it can take the equivalent of 85 gallons of diesel fuel in energy?It just doesn't make any sense!Corn is food for much of the world's population and North America is the biggest supplier.It is patently immoral to contribute to world hunger in this manner.

Why not give these corn farmers the green light to produce commercial hemp or some of the new hybrid plants that can offer a much superior ratio of ethanol per acre of land used?The answer is simple and this is an absolute fact:There is no money to be made by the chemical companies if hemp cultivation reappeared as it does not require fertilisers, pesticides or insecticides to grow and it does not deteriorate topsoil as corn does, it also can produce many fold the ethanol per acres as corn can.The bottom line is, hemp competes with too many of these super rich companies, like the paper companies, the oil companies, the cotton industry, the coal industry, the nylon, the polyester, the metal, the paint, the dynamite, the pharmaceutical etc. etc. Industrial Hemp is the world most versatile and most useful plant, it was too convenient for the competitors of this plant to have it destroyed under the pretence that it is Marijuana which is not the case at all.Hemp is virtually free of THC (an active chemical ingredient in Marijuana) while Marijuana has around 25% THC. Reports have indicated that the THC content in agriculturally grown industrial hemp is less than 2%.Hemp is not a drug and never has been.

Much can be learned by examining the similarities of how the Agricultural Hemp and Salmon Industries were destroyed by Corporations using Governments for self serving purposes.

The big question is how much longer will our governments continue to cooperate with the destroyers of our environment and how much longer will they continue to hide the facts of their involvement with the mistakes and misshapen policies of the past.These failings are so obvious now as to make governments look totally incompetent unless things will change dramatically.

I am extremely concerned for the future of my grandchildren, who are already living in an environment that is poisoned by these greedy companies and with corrupted government leaders who prefer handouts to taking the proper decisions for the best environment opportunities for its citizens?I hope this book will contribute to raising public outrage through the roof about this corruption of government policy by Big Corporate Interests.

We the human race are now dying at an alarming rate from all sorts of cancers, diabetes, heart diseases and much of this misery is entirely from our own doing of supplying our kids with low grade food and a polluted environment.The bad news is that the future does not look all that bright for increasing human life-span. Our governments are using the statistics of people over eighty years old to brainwash the public that they are now living (**today**) longer than they lived before.This is totally inaccurate as it is impossible to know how long people of **today** (born today) will live, yes people now in their eighties and over are living older than ever did before, but those people were born over eighty years ago and raised on wholesome foods, not fast food or food filled with hormones, colouring like used in fish farming, antibiotics, and a long list of chemicals. Some research indicates we have reached our maximum life-span and from now on it could very well be downhill for most of us if we do not start producing wholesome foods and de-pollute our environment.

Hopefully activists groups will concentrate their efforts on the real important issues, like deforestation, pollution of our air, of our rivers, of our lakes, of our oceans, of our land; issues affecting farming, cattle and poultry, and the safety of our food supply.

These are the issues that activists groups should be tackling, not the goals of an idealistic world of man and nature which does not and never will exist.They must stop targeting people with highly emotional propaganda, inciting them to give money that is used for creating political havoc.These groups are part of the reason we have such a polarized political system and government gridlock where urgent responses to crisis is almost impossible and civilized discussion on complex environmental issues is non-existent.

The Bottom Line . . .

The saga of this Horrendous Environmental Conspiracy has had a devastating impact on our Canadian and US economy. The losses are colossal; altogether hundreds of thousands of jobs have been and continue to be lost. It will take over a half century for our forest to re-grow and start creating substantial opportunities for our loggers and papermakers to get back to work. It will take decades before our formerly extensive and very productive cod fisheries can resume to normal and create thousands of jobs as in the past. Since the ban on seal hunting thousands of small business, restaurants, fly-shops, taxidermists, inns, salmon fishing guides and outfitters who earned a good living with the sport salmon fishing in the past have gone under. The collapse of the First Nations subsistence fisheries is a tragedy adding to this, the effects from the ban on seal and whale hunting, aboriginal communities have lost extensively from these policies.

According to Robert Cooney, historian at the time, published in 1832, A Compendious History of the Northern Part of New Brunswick and the Gaspe District. Robert Cooney evaluated at 10 000 barrels the quantity of salmon taken from the Restigouche in 1813, over 4 000 000 pounds of salmon.

Archives from the period, shows the Department of Fisheries authorised John Adams, James Duncan and Adam Ferguson each a license for netting salmon in the estuary of the Restigouche River. John Adams setup a 135 fathoms (810 yards) net in the estuary in front of what is today the City of Campbellton, and 800 yards upstream from Adams was James Duncan's setup, followed by Adam Ferguson 800 yards above Duncan's.

The cost per season license was established at a $1.00 per barrel of salmon harvested. On July the 13th 1874, John Adams came to Matapedia to report his catch to the fishery clerk Ino Mowat, (as shown in archive receipt) 12,808 barrels for station No.6, John Adams reported.

Each barrel contained between 400 to 500 lbs of salmon, it is estimated that John Adams harvested some 150,000 salmon with a single net for the 1874 season. When accounting for all of Duncan's and Ferguson's harvest, and possibly a dozen more licenses, the total harvest could have surpassed a million salmon for the 1874 season. Evidently it is conceivable that the Restigouche River Basin during the 19th century had a run of a million salmon annually and possibly as much as two million fish.

According to the North Atlantic Salmon Funds as of 1998, the **world total** Atlantic salmon population was estimated at TWO MILLION wild Atlantic salmon. For 2008 the Restigouche River Basin had a salmon run estimated at 20 to 25 000 fish, (mostly all grills) a very disappointing outcome if compared to a century ago when most salmon weighed over thirty pounds. It is very sad observing the prestige of the world greatest Atlantic Salmon River, the magnificent Restigouche River Basin, forced toward ruin due to greed and corrupted policies. The people of New Brunswick and Quebec must take back what is rightfully theirs in the first place, a natural heritage, a **Stolen Treasure.**

Most large scale polluters of the environment spend billions $$$ annually in advertizing campaigns, flooding our media with propaganda orchestrated to distract people's attention from the real environmental issues and frequently distorting scientific evidence so as to polish their corporate image and create false impressions that these corporate giants are good custodians of the environment and worth of public trust.These large scale environmental polluters generate a large percentage of the commercial media's income and one should not expect the media companies to displease their most lucrative clients.The old expression "don't bite the hand that feeds you" applies here.The bottom line is very clear...the mainstream commercial media...television and print news, does not do a very good job of researching, and reporting on the subject of environmental crimes and abuses.Only academic, and occasionally, government funded research, is published; and these get very little public circulation.It is not surprising then that the public is not properly informed about environmental issues or even the alternatives that can really help make our environment cleaner and safer.

The crushing the industrial hemp industry is a typical example, thus preventing a promising hemp industry from ever making it past the start up phase, while allowing the most prolific polluters to rake in mega profits by not having to compete against hemp products. What about diesel engines?

They pollute 40% less than gas engines and our leaders prefer talking about properly inflating our tire pressure to at best save a mere 2% on gas emissions. The possibilities are there, it should have been law years ago for all new cars and trucks manufactured to use diesel engines instead of gas engines, diesel engines consume 40% less fossil fuel than gas engines do. Then what's the problem for not introducing diesel engines as an important solution for reducing greenhouse gas emissions? It's simple, here again, it's all about money.Reducing fossil fuel sales by 40% equals to a reduction of 40% of fuel tax income for governments and 40% less fossil fuel sales for the oil companies.Hemp is not the crime!The crime is the intentional sabotage of the industrial hemp industry by large energy and chemical corporations whose huge piles of "dirty money" have corrupted government and science.Biodiesel from hemp has been shown to be a clean source of energy that can put us on the highway toward nearly zero greenhouse gas emissions.It is a proven technology that has been around for a long time; so what are we waiting for?

In the province of Manitoba it has been legal to cultivate industrial hemp for years. Manitoba farmers have been growing hemp and selling the fiber to a processing plant in California.For reasons that are unclear and highly suspicious as no warning signs were apparent, the California plant suddenly declared bankruptcy. The sudden closure of the California plant, their single largest buyer, could have financially destroyed the hemp farmers of Manitoba, but these Manitoba farmers have survived the ordeal and are now back cultivating hemp for the production of hemp milk and hemp oil for human consumption with overwhelming success. It seems that only when hemp cultivation is used for products that are **not competing** with the giant oil and chemical industry, is it **allowed** to survive.

According to numerous credible reports if governments encouraged industrial hemp to reach its full potential it could sustain indefinitely for North American's more than a million good paying jobs, a trillion dollar a year industry, total independence over foreign oil and a clean environment.

When accounting from the very beginning only for the **salmon conspiracy**, and for the next two decades at least, considering direct and indirect jobs and all monetary revenues that should have been generated by all of these activities, Canada and the US could have wasted as much as a Trillion dollars in economic losses for all of Atlantic Canada and Northern New England.Today we have very little to show in exchange for the man made destruction of our forests and rivers and we are left, not only with the cost of cleaning up after the mess, but we must now also pay even more to develop the new technologies necessary to avoid a repeat of the horrendous environmental disasters of the 20th century.

Canadians Have to Stand on Guard for Thee . . .

There is no question about it Canada is a wonderful country to live in, it is peaceful, there are abundant natural resources, good jobs, good social programs, all ideal conditions for Canadians to be laying back relaxing and enjoying the good life.This is just about what everyone is doing too.

This nonchalant attitude from Canadians too busy enjoying the good life especially during the last four decades, has given our governments a blank check to regulate big corporate industries as they pleased.It is the responsibility of these regulators to protect the best interests of the public.Instead we are tolerating a system where corporations and wealthy individuals control the regulators.If this is not corruption then I do not know the meaning of the word "corruption". We have permitted big business and their money managers to gain control of most media, one company in New Brunswick, The Irving Oil and Logging Company controls most if not all of the English media in that province. Also the Irving Company owns and controls more than half of the GDP of the province of New Brunswick; it is the largest logging company in Eastern Canada.Having total control of the media and controlling over 50% of the GDP of a province is a dangerous environment conducive for the massive abuses discussed in earlier chapters.

I am not trying to present a moral, but just to awaken your insights. Too many of us are sleeping at the switch when it comes to questioning the way our governments regulate corporate titans and their way of doing business.

We observe regularly on television news where someone somewhere is beaten up and robbed.We all condemn these acts, and we all believe that the aggressors should not get away with this behaviour and that they should be punished... But, in North America it seems readily accepted that the corporations and rich wealthy elite's who run them can use their financial or political advantages to appropriate public resources for themselves and to use mischievously cunning methods that are tolerated by our legal systems.It is always **open season** for the rich and powerful to prey on the rights and property of the working class general public.Where are the rights activist's campaigns against this very real threat to people's lives and well being?Countless incidents can be enumerated in which power is wielded by and for the sake of the almighty dollar.It seems there is no enforcement of the existing laws prohibiting the corruption of government by money.Where is the public outrage?

I have a friend who has lost his service station in a gas war, which was initiated by the big oil companies like Irving.I was just recently talking with him about it.He lost his business, his house and the financial means to send his son to college.I asked if he would rather have had one good beating brutal enough to put him in the hospital, or lose his business to the gas war.His answer was clear . . . '' **I`ll take a beating any day!** ``

One can understand how big companies like the forest industry giants, or extremely rich people like the riparian owners have a clear path to administrate themselves.There is a revolving door between government regulating agencies and the companies they regulate.Individuals working in government migrate to the corporate entities they are supposed to regulate.Corporate executives take positions in the government agencies.Corporations encourage this behaviour as it drastically compromises these individuals and blunts the effectiveness of the regulating agency. Many government employees in positions of authority who have detected these behaviours prefer to remain silent due rather than risk the dangerous implications of confronting rich and powerful offenders.

Throughout Canada, and mainly in New Brunswick and Quebec, there is no possible means of airing views on forestry management especially scientific information which can demonstrate its effects on salmon rivers, lakes, streams and its massive impact (responsible for 25%) on Canada's greenhouse effect. Access to newspaper, TV or Radio broadcasts is being denied to Canadian citizens if it has anything to do with the effect of logging. The right to free speech inscribed in our constitution, and our prized democratic system is being denied to Canadians. No less of a distinguished personality than documentary film maker David Suzuki has been prevented by national media from exposing the illegal forestry practices in Canada.

(Read letter below)

The point is, still in 2008 our legal system tolerates big business using their financial powers to corrupt the leaders of our federations and foundations.Our government system is even supplying these rich individuals with the benefits of tax deductible loop-holes like the Restigouche Salmon Club Scholarship Program.Please understand that I have no objection to college scholarships for anyone.However, just imagine the scenario of walking into any small community Town Hall along the Restigouche River Basin and saying to some of the local authorities:"You know our fishing club are darn good people, they'd do anything to help you.If you have a son or daughter going to college, we want to help out. We know that it can cost a leg and an arm for parents living way out here to send their kids to college. How about we give your kids a scholarship of $5,000.00 each?"Up to this point I have no problem whatsoever with the "program".I have problems with the "pay-back" which comes much later on.Don't you think that it is conceivable that the riparian property taxes will not increase by a single penny for years to come, or even not be taxed at all which is the case on many of our Salmon River basins?

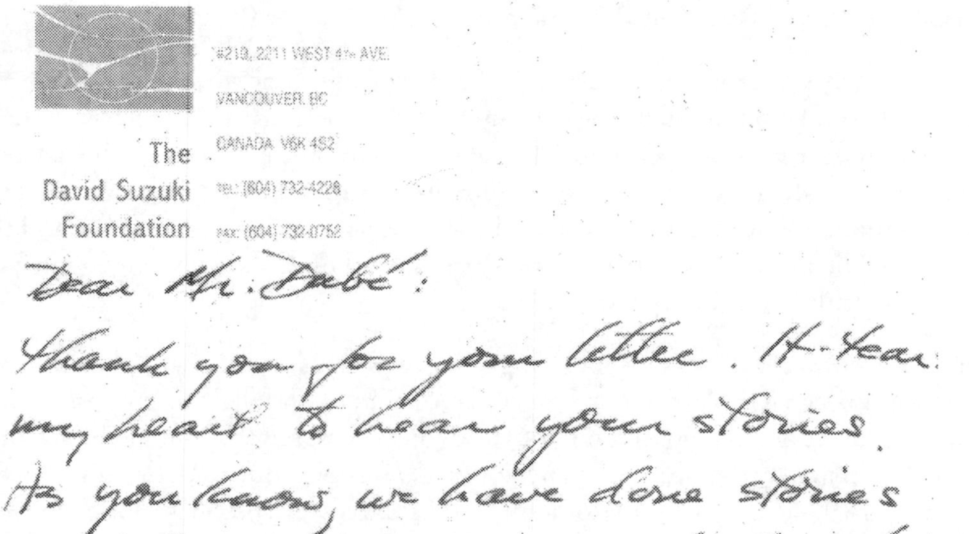

The David Suzuki Foundation

#219, 2211 West 4th Ave.
Vancouver, BC
Canada V6K 4S2
tel: (604) 732-4228
fax: (604) 732-0752

Dear Mr. Dubé:

Thank you for your letter. It tears my heart to hear your stories. As you know, we have done stories on clearcut logging and have been hammered by the forest industry. Right now the CBC is under siege and terrified of getting into more controversy. It's sure

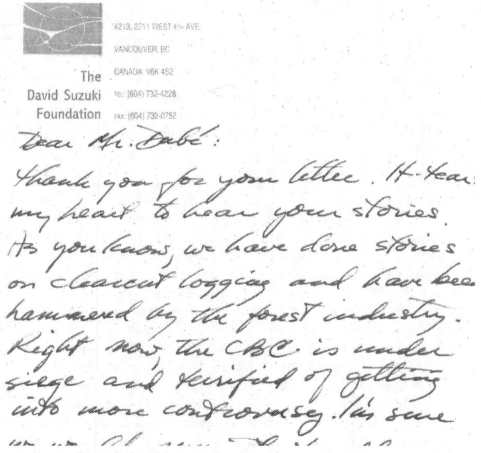

And to top it all, it's all tax deductible, compliments of our governments . . . is this great country or what?How can we continue to be so stupid as to exchange a few small handouts in return for withholding property tax assessments on hundreds of millions of dollars of real estate owned by

the wealthiest people in North America?This revenue is desperately needed by the people of the provinces who are absorbing the cost of this outrageous subsidy.All these outcomes perpetuate a permanent state of near poverty and depression for the area and a ready source of cheap seasonal labour for the Lords of the Restigouche.

Governments have allowed the rich and powerful to set the agenda as they please.Companies and their executive puppets have taken every opportunity to assume control of key foundations and federations entering through the backdoor and hiding behind an appearance of public service as market propaganda to an unknowing public and influence government policy for their own benefit; in effect raping us of our natural resources.How can we trust a government that lets things like this happen and then pretends that these foundations and federations are actually functioning in the public interest? . . . Where is the public outrage?

Meetings of the Directors and Members of some of the Federations and Foundations I am speaking about reveal a good example of the kind of individuals we are dealing with. I have observed these corporate elite's at such meetings.Guys who have participated in the destruction of our salmon rivers, polluted our waterways, strut about while attending these annual reunions and often accept plaques and awards for good citizenship and environmental responsibility.Heads high, shoulders back, they look fellow anglers straight in the eye confidently knowing the regular members do not have a clue of what is really going on behind the scenes.Academy Awards could be given out to these people for "Most Fraudulent Performance by a Politician or Business Mogul".

Many anglers have asked me frequently . . . ′′ Aren't you afraid of what these people might do to you because of your stand in informing the public of their actions? `` The answer is no, I am not afraid of them.In fact it is they who should be afraid, not of me, but because the day of reckoning is fast approaching when they will be held accountable for their horrendous environmental crimes and the corruption of government.It is an informed public that they are afraid of and they should be.They fear public outrage and the reforms which will follow.Closer investigations into financial dealings could result in criminal prosecutions.

Everyone has their personal reasons for doing things so I will confess that I also have my own axe to grind in this matter. My place of business suffered millions of dollars in property damage due to (**man-made**) sources of ice flooding from the Restigouche River in the Matapedia sector.Adding to this was the extensive economic losses to my outfitting business due to poor salmon runs after the seal hunt ban in 1974.I began a series of legal actions to recover compensation for these damages, and in that process, was able to discover much of the information that is set forth in this book.The pieces of the puzzle started coming together causing me to realize that a horrendous environmental conspiracy has taken place here in Eastern Canada. The conspiracy was mustered up mainly by the Irving Company for obvious reasons explained earlier, who along with certain other of their fellow riparian rights owning pals have subverted and dominated the Public Interest Foundations, using this cover to influence government policy and rule making so as to benefit their own private objective which is to maintain their own private and exclusive use of the fabulous Atlantic Salmon fishing waters of the Restigouche drainage. It is perfectly clear that the Irving's have a long history of getting their way in New Brunswick.They are so large and so concentrated in this economically distressed province that they are a law unto themselves.Most government officials there have a real fear of challenging the Irving cartel.I fully expect this situation will change as soon as the general public becomes informed that primary reason that the economy of New Brunswick is in such bad shape is because these citizens have been living with the results of a corrupted government and an economic system that is a throwback to feudal times (one major landlord surrounded by a few loyal administrators keeping a firm hand on sources of power and wealth while at the same time allowing just enough economic benefits to trickle down to the people who form an underclass of employees whose lives are in the hand of their employer).

Stopping the seal hunt devastated tens of thousands of people's livelihood including all businesses and individuals earning their living from Atlantic Salmon sport fishing which was my case. I absolutely felt then that I had the moral responsibility to denounce these gangsters, when knowing very well that no one would do it if I didn't. Just the simple fact of knowing that these individuals had allowed our salmon rivers; our forests; our lakes; our waterways; our oceans and the livelihood of ten's of thousands of good honest residents living on the Atlantic Coast to be destroyed and would get away with it, this was absolutely unacceptable for me to let that happen.

I so often hear from old salmon anglers, saying we do not understand why anglers can not content themselves with one or two Atlantic salmon for three or four days of fishing. I can understand that these old anglers come now for "the fishing" not the fish, they need to understand also and realise when they started fishing in their younger days, they were catching all kinds of salmon, and that is the main reason they got hooked on salmon fishing in the first place.Today young anglers starting to fish for salmon in Eastern Canada often have to fish for many days or weeks, sometime seasons, before catching a single salmon, and most likely their first catch will be a grill. This explains why the average young anglers get discouraged early on and abandon fishing for Atlantic salmon.This does not apply to the very few and fortunate young anglers who happen to be lucky enough to have access to riparian owned waters that always have much more salmon to be caught.Young salmon anglers are on the downward slide and the present salmon anglers are getting older by the seasons, but, the riparian owners (The Atlantic Salmon Federation as well as the Quebec Salmon Federation) certainly do not seem to be the least concerned or alarmed by this fact . . .I wonder why?

Recapitulating . . .

1608 to 1960 French Quebecquers have one of, if not the highest birth-rate in the world, with very few college graduates, while English Quebecquers not under the total dominance of the catholic religion like the French were having moderate birth-rate and could afford college educations. While French Quebecquers, who formed the backbone of the labouring class, were fully occupied with seventy hour plus work weeks and supporting these very large families.This situation which persisted for nearly 300 years left French speaking peoples with little leisure time to capitalize on their great hunting and fishing heritage.This situation was eagerly exploited by others who grabbed control of entire forest lands and river systems and privatized these areas for their personal benefits. All others including French Speaking Quebecquers were virtually locked out from accessing much of the prime forest land and rivers in Quebec and completely locked out of New Brunswick.

1965 French Quebecquers are rapidly moving toward one of the lowest birth-rates in the world and are soon to be counted among the most educated people in the country.

1968 the first separatist party is formed with René Levesque as its leader, promising to do away with all private hunting and fishing clubs in the province of Quebec.

1970 the Irving Whales goes down in the Gulf of St-Lawrence and J. D. Irving admits later that there was 7.2 tons of highly toxic PCB's on board. (We will never know exactly how many tons of PCB s was really on board, 7.2 tons is what the Irving Company declared.) There is strong suspicion that there was much more than just the 7.2 tons Irving admitted.

1971 the year before the band of commercial netting in the Bay des Chaleurs Newfoundland and Labrador, the government of Quebec sells approximately 5,000 **resident** salmon season licenses annually and just a little more for moose hunting season licenses.

1972 the Board of Directors of the ASA (Atlantic Salmon Association) who were at that time composed of some non riparian individuals (but still under the dominance of the riparian owners) that pressured the ASA to accomplish the major goal of having all the commercial nets taken out of the Bay des Chaleurs, Newfoundland and Labrador and all our rivers filled up plumb full with many GIANT Atlantic salmon.

1974 Quebec's total sales of salmon season licenses skyrocketed to over 26,000 from about 8,000 just three years earlier in 1971, (the year before the lifting of the commercial nets).So many new **resident** Atlantic salmon anglers obviously presented a serious threat to the idea of private fishing right and the riparian rights owners knew something needed to be done if they wanted to hold-on to their private fishing paradise.

1974 the seal hunt is stopped following an unprecedented media travesty orchestrated by activist groups who paid seal hunters to put on a blood soaked show of clubbing and skinning white seal pups in front of the cameras.Even though the activities that were filmed bore no resemblance to real seal hunting, public outrage world-wide escalated and seal hunting was banned by law.

1976 the most powerful fishing club in the world the Restigouche Salmon Club loses all of its Red Bank private fishing waters. The clubs of the Restigouche River and riparian owners of other rivers like the Cascapedia, the Moisie, the Bonaventure just to name a few were all under siege and at risk of losing their private salmon fishing waters to the de-clubbing moment led by the so called "Second French Revolution" and the threatened separation of Quebec from Canada.

1977 the beluga whales are dying with cancer and their reproductive rate has dramatically declined in the Gulf of St-Lawrence, caused by contamination of the gulf with PAH (polycylic aromatic hydrocarbons) from aluminum smelters and PCB's most likely from the Irving Whale fiasco. There are also warning signs that something is going wrong with the Atlantic Coast Cod fishery.

1982 the cod fishery is well on its way of a total collapse, and over harvesting is not the main cause of the depletions of the Atlantic cod.The downhill slide of the cod stocks coincides very precisely with the increase of the seal populations which was in 1974 estimated at 600,000 strong, is today estimated at over ten millions just on Canada's East Cast.(By 1992 it was all over for the cod fishery, it was closed down due to the total collapse of the Atlantic stock.Ten's of thousands of people lost their livelihood.)

1982 Atlantic Salmon populations have also been decimated by the stoppage of the seal hunt. It then became possible for the Foundations and Federations to influence the Government to adopt Catch & Release regulations due to Atlantic Salmon being then considered endangered species. Under the pretence of protecting salmon, Catch & Release became the rule of law for Atlantic

Canada.The demand for Salmon licenses dramatically falls and Restigouche owners have saved their private fishing waters.

Throughout all these years and despite all these issues, the private fishing pools of the Restiqouche have always provided very good fishing.It is my profound belief that if the time ever comes when the last surviving Atlantic Salmon comes home, that fish will die alone in the fabulousMillion Dollar Pool on the Restigouche River.

2008 Atlantic salmon returns show signs of improvement, (Was it a coincidence our salmon runs have increased in 2008, or was it the document sent to the premier of New Brunswick pressuring the ASF to clean up their act?) but even these measurements promote a false sense of accomplishment.Comparing the improved 2008 Salmon returns to the returns of 2007 (which was one of the lowest on record) is self congratulatory puffery.The Salmon situation is in trouble from many directions. Damage to the riverbed habitats and high water temperature is getting worse. The Salmon returns of many rivers have remained unchanged and many rivers barely meet their conservation requirements.And the cod fishery... after all those years of protection, one would have to believe that the North Atlantic should now be plumb full of Cod. Nothing much has changed there either as Cod populations have made a very limited recovery defying the predictions of the government scientists.

2008 the status-quo for the North Atlantic remains the same ...

Right now my thoughts consist of a number of serious questions which are disturbing to say the least.

Are we seeing the end of an era?

Are we seeing the middle class of North America disappearing, crushed by the steamroller of giant corporations?

When is the public going to say enough is enough, and demand that governments be accountable and take responsibility for their actions and decisions?

Will Canadians and Americans respond to this alarming situation?Will they take concrete action, or remain passive?

Will they write their elected representatives, requesting immediate action to save the North Atlantic Fisheries and the rivers of Eastern Canada?

Will they examine the leadership and directors of their Atlantic Salmon Federations and Conservation groups to reform conflicts of these director's business interests with the public interests of the Federations.Will the Foundations and Federations ever move forward, and tackle the difficult issues of water quality and forestry practices and ocean predator management.

Will the Foundations and Federations take an active role in supporting Atlantic Salmon fishing rights for everyone, including aboriginal peoples, as opposed to continuing their protection and promotion of the private fishing rights for a few.

I hope the readers have recognized in this paper the urgent action required to save what I consider to be the loss of prestige our famous salmon rivers are suffering.

What causes the general population to be so very passive with regard to the desecration of all we have ever known about our heritage?

Why should a few Corporate Tycoons be allowed to use their financial powers to rob us of this wonderful natural heritage.

When will people stand up and be counted? Why do we always wait until it is too late?

Remember These Rules:

One Lie Always Leads to Another.

Nothing is more important than the Truth.

Figures Don't Lie but Liars Figure.

Question Authority. Things are Often Not as They Appear.

Always Follow the Trail of Money to the Source.

Power Corrupts and Absolute Power Corrupts Absolutely.

Money is the source of all evil.

Forgive but Never Forget.

Fool Me Once, Shame on You.

Fool Me Twice, Shame on Me.

The author while guiding a young American angler with a GIANT Restigouche salmon

Literature Sighted and Consulted

Alexander, Robert R. 1974.Silviculture of the central and southern Rocky Mountain forest:A summary of the status of our knowledge by timber types.

UDSA For. Serv. RES. PAP. Rm - 120, 36P. ROCKY Mt. For. And Range Exp. Stn., Fort Collins, Colo. Barr, George W. 1956.

Recovering rainfall. Part 1, Arizona Watershed Program.Cooperating: Arizona State Land Dep., Water Div., Salt River Valley Users Assoc., Univ. of Ariz. 33p Bates C. G., and A. J. Henry. 1928.

Forest and stream flow experiment at Wagon Wheel Gap., Colorado. Mon., Weather Rev. Suppl. 30, 79p. Brown, Harry E. 1970.

Status of watershed studies in Arizona.Am. Soc. Eng., J. Irrig. Drain. Div., 96 (1R1): 11-23. Brown, H. E., and J. R. Thompson 1965.

Summer water use by aspen, spruce, and grassland in western Colorado. J. For. 63:756-760. Copeland. Otis L. 1969.

Forest Service Research in erosion control.Trans. Am. Soc. Civil Eng. 12 (1): 75-79. Eakins, Henry M. 1936.

Silting of reservoirs U.S. Dep. Tech. Bull. 524 168p. (Rev. 1939). Fletcher, H.C., and L.R. Rich. 1955

Classifying south-western watersheds on the basis of water yield,. J. For. 53:196-202, Forsling. C. L. 1960.

Watershed management to increase water yield.Water Conf. Proc. N. M. State Univ., Las Cruses, Nov. 5:62-66. Gay. Floyd W. 1971.

Forest climatology at, Oregon State University, Sel. Paps. 29th Annu. Meet., Proc. Oreg. Acad. Sci. 7:77-23.Goodell, Bertanm C. 1958.

A preliminary report on the first year`s effects of timber harvesting on the water yield from a Colorado watershed. US. Dep. Pap. 36, 12p. Fort Collins. Colo. Hibbert, Alden R. 1966.

Forest treatment effects on water yield. P. 527-543, In Int. Symp. For. Hydrol. Proc., Aug. 29-Sept. 10, 1965, Pa. State Univ. Park Hoover, M.D. 1944.

Effect of removal of forest vegetation upon water yield.Trans. Am. Geophys. Union 25:969=975. Hoover, Marvin D., and Charles F. Leaf. 1966.

Process and significance of interception in Colorado subalpine forest. P. 213-224, IN Int. Symp. For Hydrol. Proc., Aug. 29-Sept. 10 1965. Pa. State UNIV., Univ. Park. Horton, Jerome S., and C. J. Campbell. 1974.

Management of phreatophyte and riparian vegetation for maximum multiple use values. USDA For. Serv. Res. Pap. RM-117, 23p. Rocky Mt. For. And Range Exp. Stn., Fort Collins, Colo. Horbeck, J. W., R. S. Pierce, and C.A. Federer. 1970.

Streamflow changes after clearing forest in New England.Water Resolur.Res. 6:1124-1132. Hoyt, W. G., and H. C. Froxell. 1934.

Forest and streamflow. Trans Am. Soc. Civil Eng. 99:1-111. Johnson, E. A., and J. L. Kovner. 1956.

Effect on streamflow of cutting forest understory. For. Sci. 2:82-91 Kelso, Maurice M., William E. Martin, and Lawrence E. Mack. 1973.

Water supplies and economic growth in an arid environment, an Arizona case study. Univ. Ariz. Press. 327p. Tucson, Kovner , Jacob L. 1956.

Evapotranspiration and water yield following forest cutting and natural regrowth. Proc. Soc. Am., Memphis, Tenn. P. 106-110.Kramer, Paul J. 1969.

Plant and soil water relationships: A modern synthesis. 482p. McGraw-Hill Book Co., N.Y. Leaf, Charles F. 1966.

Sediment yield from high mountain watersheds, central Colorado. US. For. SER. Res. Pap. RM-23 15p. Rocky Mt. For and Range Exp. Stn., Fort Collins, Colo. Leaf. Charles F. 1972.

Simulating watershed management practices in Colorado subalpine forest. Am. Soc. Civil Eng. Annu. and Natl. Environ. Eng. Meet. Houston. Tex., Oct. 16-22. Prepr. 1840, 26p Lewis, David C. 1968.

Annual hydrologic response to watershed conversion from oak-woodland to annual grassland.Water Resour. Res. 4:59-72. Love, L.D. 1955.

The effect on stream flow on the dilling of spruce and pine by the Engelmann spruce beetle.Trans. Am. Geophys. Union, 36:113-118.Mc Guinness, J. L., and L. L. Harold. 1971.

Reforestation influence on small watershed streamflow.Water Resour. Res. 7:845-852. McNaughton, K. G., and F. A. Black. 1973.

A study of evapotranspiration from a Douglas-fir forest using the energy balance approach.Water Resour. Res. 9:1579-1590.Martinelli, M., Jr. 1964.

Watershed management in the Rocky Mountain alpine and subalpine zones.U.S. For. Serv. Res. Note RM-36, 7p. Rocky Mt. For. And Ranges Exp. Stn., Fort Collins. Colo. Patric, James H., and Kenneth G. Reinhart. 1971.

Hydrologic effect of deforestation two mountain watersheds in West Virginia,Water Resour. Res. 7:1182-1188. Rich, L. R. 1962.

Erosion and sediment movement following a wildfire in a ponderosa pine forest of central Arizona. U.S. Dep. Agric., For. Serv., Note 76, 12p. Fort Collins, Colo. Rich, Lowell Rr. 1972.

Managing a ponderosa pine forest to increase water yield.Water Resour. Res. 8:422-428. Rich, L.R., H. R., H. G. Reynolds, and A. J. West. 1961.

The Workman Creek experimental watershed. U.S. Dep. Agric. For. Ser., Rocky Mt. For. And Range Exp. Stn. Pap. 65, 18p. Fort Collins, Colo. Rothacher. Jack. 1965.

Streamflow from small watershed in the western slope of the Cascade Range of Oregon.Water Resour. Res. 9:125-134.Rothacker, Jack. 1970.

Increase in water yield following clear-cut logging in the Pacific Northwest.Water Resour. Res. 6:653-658.Tennyson, Larry C. 1973.

Snowfall interception in Arizona ponderosa pine forests.Master's Thesis. 56p. Dep. Of Watershed Nage., Univ. of ARIZ. Thompson, J. R. 1974.

Energy budget measurements over three cover types in eastern Arizona. Water Resour. Res. 10:145-1048.

Restigouche River study: ASSE Consultants Inc. and Hare Fisheries & Environmental Consultants Inc. March 1992.

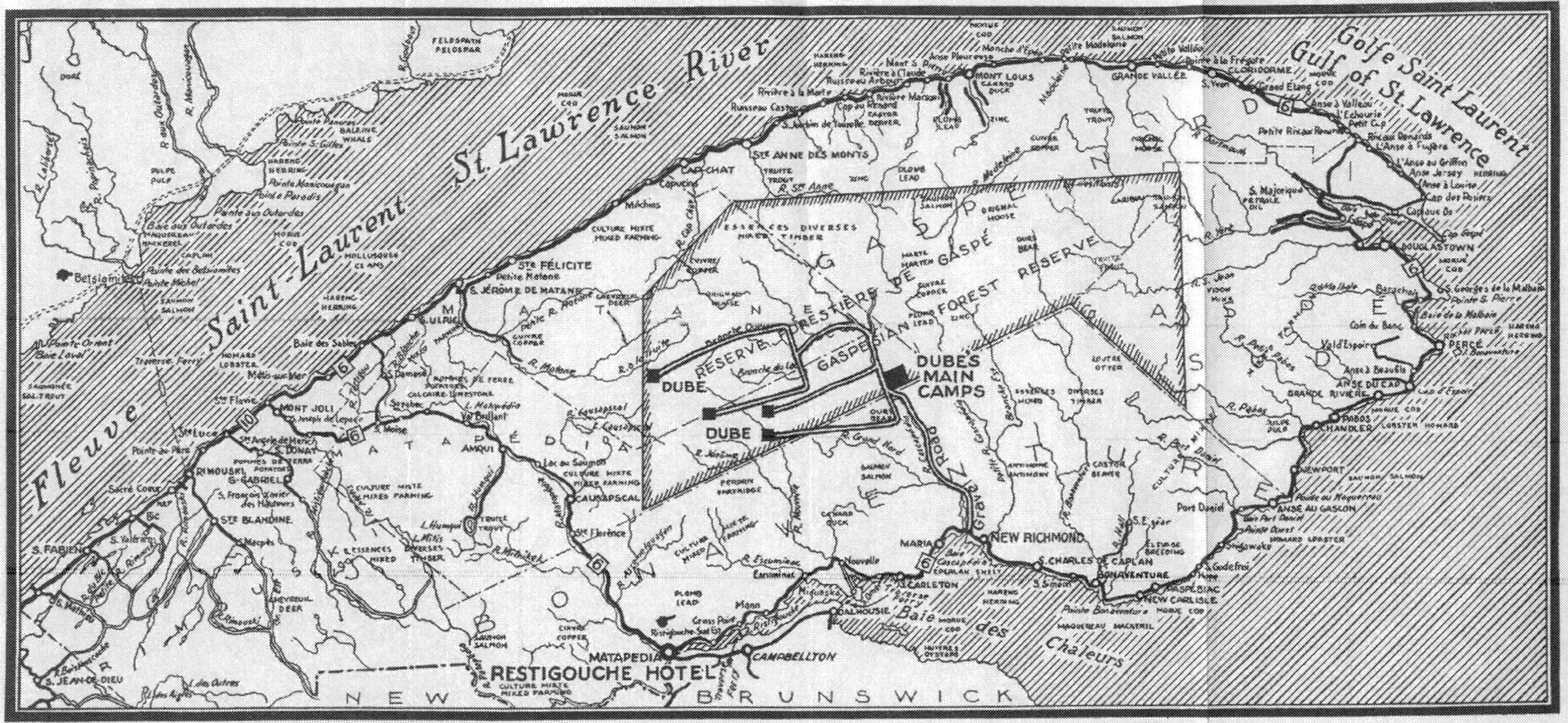
Fleuve Saint-Laurent
St. Lawrence River
Golfe Saint Laurent
Gulf of St. Lawrence
Baie des Chaleurs
NEW BRUNSWICK
RESTIGOUCHE HOTEL
MATAPEDIA
CAMPBELLTON
DUBES MAIN CAMPS
DUBE
DUBE
RESERVE
GASPESIAN FOREST RESERVE
FORESTIÈRE DE GASPÉ
Gravel Road
NEW RIMOUSKI
MONT JOLI
AMQUI
CAUSAPSCAL
STE FÉLICITE
CAP CHAT
STE ANNE DES MONTS
MONT LOUIS
GRANDE VALLÉE
DOUGLASTOWN
PERCÉ
CHANDLER
NEW RICHMOND
MARIA
CARLETON
BONAVENTURE
NEW CARLISLE
NEWPORT
ANSE AU GASCON
GRANDE RIVIÈRE
PABOS
DALHOUSIE
RIMOUSKI
S. GABRIEL
STE BLANDINE
S. FABIEN
S. JEAN-DE-DIEU
S. CHARLES DE CAPLAN
PASPÉBIAC
Betsiamis
CLORIDORME

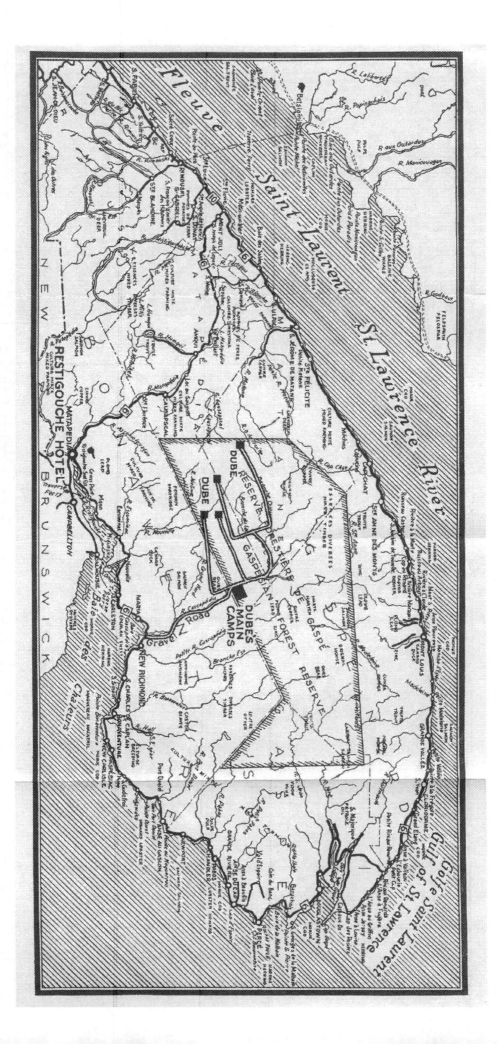